Labor History Collection

Madison Area Technical
College Teachers' Union
Local 243

Printed by MATC, Local 3872

Labor at
the Ballot Box

The Massachusetts

Prevailing Wage

Campaign of 1988

Labor and Social Change,

a series edited by Paula Rayman and Carmen Sirianni

Labor at the Ballot Box

The Massachusetts

Prevailing Wage

Campaign of 1988

Mark Erlich

 Temple University Press | Philadelphia

Temple University Press, Philadelphia 19122
Copyright © 1990 by Temple University. All rights reserved
Published 1990
Printed in the United States of America

∞ The paper used in this publication meets the minimum
requirements of American National Standard for Information
Sciences—Permanence of Paper for Printed Library Materials,
ANSI Z39.48-1984

Library of Congress Cataloging-in-Publication Data

Erlich, Mark, 1949-
Labor at the ballot box : the Massachusetts prevailing wage
campaign of 1988 / Mark Erlich.
p.   cm.—(Labor and social change)
ISBN 0-87722-727-6 (alk. paper)
1. Trade-unions—Massachusetts—Political activity.   2. Working
class—Massachusetts—Political activity.   3. Wages—Building
trades—Massachusetts.   4. Public contracts—Massachusetts.
I. Title. II. Series.
HD8079.M4E75   1990
322'.2'09744—dc20   89-20631
                                                               CIP

To my parents

Contents

Illustrations

ix

Preface

THIS BOOK is the story of a political campaign. It covers the standard elements of a modern-day campaign, for example, polling data, media strategy, voter registration, field operations, telephone banking, and get-out-the-vote plans. But the intent of this narrative is to go beyond contemporary political buzzwords and examine what made the effort to preserve the prevailing wage law in Massachusetts in 1988 something other than a strictly conventional electoral campaign.

Voters were asked either to repeal or preserve a state law governing wages on publicly funded construction sites in Massachusetts. There was no "candidate." Because a referendum question was involved, the nature of the campaign was, of necessity, more issue oriented than most candidate elections. While the personal popularity of public figures associated with either side of the debate may have been a contributing factor, individual voters' decisions typically depended on the effectiveness of the case built by proponents or opponents of the ballot measure.

The campaign broke through the minimal voter concern that characterizes many referendum contests. In an election year that included a presidential race featuring the state's governor, the battle over Question 2 generated at least as much interest as any other item on the ballot. In addition, the campaign involved thousands of rank-and-file union members who personalized issues of substance in a way that is foreign to the standard campaign defined by political consultants and television sound-bites.

The effort to defeat Question 2 represented a genuine, if sometimes fragile, labor–community coalition that is often sought but rarely achieved. Campaign themes that emphasized protecting and extending the quality of life in working communities clearly struck a resonant chord in light of the sharp class-based divisions of the election returns. As a cautionary note, however, I believe it is inappropriate to draw far-reaching conclusions on the basis of one campaign centered on one relatively obscure issue. The long-term impact on the building trades unions or the rest of the mainstream labor movement in Massachusetts remains to be measured. Unfortunately, as we head into the 1990s, the multitude of causes that have weakened organized labor in the United States as a factor in social and economic policy are still firmly in place. The corporate offensive of the last two decades shows no signs of letting up. On labor's side, questions of union militance and democracy as well as a consistent commitment to social change are still to be answered. Nonetheless, the effectiveness of this particular electoral appeal to a wide range of working people in Massachusetts should offer suggestive lessons for those attempting to craft a majoritarian progressive politics in the United States.

This book is not the handiwork of a neutral reporter—if there is such a person. I have been a union carpenter since 1973. A victory for Question 2 would have had an immediate and depressing impact on wages for all building trades workers, starting with those in the union sector of the construction industry. As a longtime labor activist, there was no question which side I was on. In the early stages of the campaign, I was one of the many unionists who worked days on a construction site and volunteered during my free time. For the final seven weeks before Election Day, I worked full time on the campaign as a statewide field coordinator. Since then, I have taken a union staff position. This is, therefore, an "insider's" account from a partisan point of view. Still, I have made every effort to present the story in a balanced historical and political context. I have tried to maintain a critical perspective and point out the campaign's flaws, foibles, and limitations. It is up to the reader to determine whether I succeeded or failed.

As a piece of political journalism, this book relies on campaign materials, newspaper accounts, and other relevant historical and contemporary documentary evidence. I have also incorporated the comments of dozens of participants in the campaign, from the leadership to activist members. Ultimately, Question 2 was defeated in the trenches through the extensive participation of rank-and-file union members. I have sought to invoke that perspective throughout my account.

I owe thanks to many people who helped this book come together. The officers and staff of the Massachusetts AFL-CIO and the Massachusetts Building Trades Council provided information and support. I would like to single out Joan Donovan and Ann-Marie Hynes in particular. I am grateful to the many people I interviewed for their time. The list of those who contributed one way or another to the campaign is nearly endless. For each person I found the time to interview, another dozen could easily have provided even more useful insights; I am sorry I missed them, and, ultimately, my thanks go to all of the participants, for they made the campaign a success.

It should be clear that those who provided me with help cannot be held accountable for any of the conclusions drawn in this book. For better or worse, I bear complete responsibility for the opinions expressed here. Incidentally, quotations in the text that are not cited in the notes are drawn from personal interviews. And, finally, in the spirit of the coalition that guided the campaign to defeat Question 2, all royalties derived from sales of this book will be donated to organizations advocating affordable housing in Massachusetts.

Labor at
the Ballot Box

The Massachusetts

Prevailing Wage

Campaign of 1988

1 | Introduction

Workers in the building trades generally wake up early. Rising before dawn, they put on their sweatshirts, work pants, and steel-toed boots, ready to be on the job at 7 A.M. November 8, 1988, was a cold, gray day, like most late fall mornings in New England, and, as usual, thousands of construction workers arrived on time at their assigned locations. That particular Tuesday was unusual, however. That day those construction workers were not wearing work clothes, and they did not pick up their customary tools once the day began.

Election Day 1988 was an unofficial holiday for union building trades workers in Massachusetts. Construction sites across the state were silent—no noisy cranes, no ringing hammers. For on that day the union men and women who build Massachusetts gathered at the polling places in the state's 351 towns and cities in an effort to persuade voters to turn down one of the referendum issues on the ballot. That day the tools of the trade were not hammers, pliers, and shovels, but signs, campaign literature, and a friendly appeal, "Please vote No on Question 2."

The operation at the polls was the culmination of a long and exhausting campaign not only for construction workers, but also for their families, other trade unionists, and the significant number of supporters who emerged in every community. For months before and after work and on weekends, campaign volunteers held signs at busy intersections, distributed leaflets, staffed phone banks, attended community meetings, and spoke to their neighbors about the importance of defeating Question 2.

"It seemed like there were a million of us out there by 7 A.M. on Election Day," remembers Bill Ryan, who served as one of the campaign's regional coordinators. "The coverage was so complete, it was eerie." The extent of the participation varied from town to town, but overall, as a Worcester newspaper put it, a "small army" of people greeted voters across the state with the "Vote No on 2" message.[1] In Abington, for example, a town with just six thousand registered voters, eighty-five volunteers stood shifts at the polls. Many worked a four-hour stint. Others were at the polls the full thirteen hours and then stayed as long as it took to get the results. Beverly carpenter Bill Conlon recalls "one retired guy with a heart condition who was there the whole day except for an hour when he went home to take his nitroglycerin."

After the last vote had been cast, poll workers gathered at election-night parties across the state or settled into their couches at home to await the outcome. At 9:53 P.M. news anchor Chet Curtis of Channel 5, Boston's ABC-TV affiliate, announced the first returns on the state's four referendum questions. With 51 precincts reporting, Curtis indicated that Question 2 would win by a margin of 55 to 45 percent. "It looks like the law is going to be repealed," he indicated. Opponents of the ballot question were stunned. The typically warm voter response to campaign workers had created expectations of a victory. Channel 5's report contradicted this admittedly unscientific but nonetheless widely shared feeling. Now it seemed that all the effort put into defeating the referendum might have been for naught.

Campaign staffers at Election Day state headquarters, located in Plumbers Local 12's union hall in Boston, discounted the television report. By 9:53 they were confidently predicting the referendum would go down to defeat by a 59 to 41 percent vote.* The superior information-gathering ability of the Committee for Quality of Life (the official name of the "Vote No on 2" campaign organization) was an outgrowth of its remarkable field organization—one of the most extensive that had ever been developed for a statewide political candidate or issue in Massachusetts.

Campaign volunteers at every polling place in the state called in the final tallies as soon as they were ready. At headquarters, a computerized operation totaled the results while separating out key predictor precincts representing a cross-section of the general population. Two hours after the polls closed, the Committee for Quality of Life's grass-roots organization of political novices had outperformed the high-tech sophistication of the wire services, radio and television outlets, and the professional political community. Channel 5's error is not significant in itself. As the wire services fed the station further results, the newscasters soon reversed their prediction. But the Committee for Quality of Life's ability to stay a step ahead of seasoned political observers through its mobilization of sheer people-power was typical of the entire campaign.

It was the maiden political voyage for the vast majority of these union members and their first taste of the potential impact of a mobilized labor community. "I know some people who had never taken a

*The final count was 58 to 42 percent.

4

day off unless they were paid," laughs Richard Bolling, a Boston ironworker. But these same people, he notes, "were out there every day. That told me something." Other campaign volunteers echo Bolling's sentiments. "I've never been involved in anything like this campaign," remarks Jack Getchell, a young officer of a bricklayers' union in New Bedford. "You'd have to go to a graveyard to find many labor people who did anything similar."

Getchell's comments reflect a common perception. While few would question the dynamism and militancy of turn-of-the-century American labor or the industrial union upsurge of the 1930s, many observers outside as well as inside organized labor have become convinced that unions are spent as an activist and progressive social force. Certainly the policies of the Reagan years only served to weaken the labor movement further. A string of legal, political, and organizational defeats dating back to the mid-1970s boxed unions into an increasingly marginal role in American political life. One-time friends of labor made political hay out of deriding unions as "special interests" that represented a shrinking percentage of the work force and were out of touch with their own membership. As A. A. Michelson, a political editor from western Massachusetts, wrote less than two weeks before the election: "Experience shows that labor leaders simply cannot deliver the votes of their members."[2]

The campaign to defeat Question 2 represented an alternate tradition and recognition that the tactics that swelled the ranks of labor in 1888 and 1938 may be just as appropriate in 1988 and beyond. Paul Roche, a twenty-nine-year-old electrician, was drawn into the campaign gradually. "I've been one of those people that sometimes looked at the labor movement as a corporation where decisions are made exclusively by leaders. The campaign brought the unions back to their members." As a ward coordinator, Roche ultimately spent all his free time in September, October, and the first week of November poring over street maps in order to design and delegate responsibilities for the 13 precincts in Boston's Ward 19. Steve Joyce, a thirty-one-year-old carpenter, was Roche's partner. "We were able to combat the 'special interest' notion," he says, "by demonstrating that we have the well-being of the entire community in mind."

The campaign not only motivated and energized trade unionists, it also dominated the state's political season. In an op-ed essay in the *Wall Street Journal*, conservative Boston journalist David Wilson affirmed what everyone could plainly see: "The hottest issue in Massachusetts as Election Day approaches is not whether Governor Michael S. Dukakis will become president or even whether Ted Kennedy will be reelected. It's Question 2. . . . Blue-and-white bumper stickers and signs bearing [the Vote No on Question 2] message appeared more than two months ago and are now, after the autumn leaves, the most prominent feature of the landscape."[3]

The issue that galvanized thousands of working men and women up to and on Election Day was the proposed repeal of the state's "prevailing wage" law. Passed in 1914, this piece of legislation requires building contractors to pay employees on state-financed projects a predetermined wage. The rates are based on local union agreements, varying by trade and geographical jurisdiction. The law stabilizes labor costs in the notoriously chaotic construction industry by fixing the pay scales that all employers— union and non-union alike—must incorporate in their bids.

For decades, the uncontroversial state prevailing wage statutes and their federal counterpart, the Davis-Bacon Act, have been of interest only to participants in the construction industry. In the last ten years, however, these once-obscure regulations have become a central battleground in the escalating employer war on American trade unions. While spearheading the effort to repeal prevailing wage laws, the Associated Builders and Contractors (ABC), an anti-union organization of construction companies, has been supported and sponsored by a wide array of high-powered employer associations and conservative organizations with an interest in eliminating the influence of all organized labor. In their eyes, an electoral victory in Massachusetts would have gone a long way toward achieving their common goal of a "union-free environment" in the United States. In June of 1988, Lawrence Allen, president of the Massachusetts/Rhode Island chapter of the ABC, confidently predicted that repeal "in Massachusetts will set a precedent with national implications."[4]

When the ABC presented 67,193 certified signatures to the secretary of state's office in the name of the Fair Wage Committee in December 1987, the conventional political wisdom was that its referendum was a shoo-in. The ABC intended to frame the issue in terms of tax savings and to this end enlisted the support of Barbara Anderson, the widely known leader of the Citizens for Limited Taxation (CLT), which had been the moving force behind successful tax-cutting referenda in 1980 and 1986. "Until Question 2," comments Jim Braude, executive director of the Tax Equity Alliance of Massachusetts, "the assumption was that anything associated with Anderson's name was invincible."

The ABC shrewdly adopted the pseudo-populist stance of the CLT and other stalking-horses of the deregulation-happy New Right. Their message was, in the words of Michael Goldman, a political consultant who stood outside the Question 2 debate, "anti-labor, anti-big, anti-anything."[5] "The common wisdom among the wise guys at the State House and even in the labor movement was that [the prevailing wage law] was gone," says Arthur Osborn, president of the Massachusetts AFL-CIO and chairman of the Committee for Quality of Life. "But I felt if we could put the people together, we could win. In some ways, it didn't matter. It involved a union principle; we had to do it."

Osborn's optimism was not widely shared. In the winter of 1987–88, the prospects for defeating the ballot question looked grim. While anti-union rhetoric may not have been as wildly popular in Massachusetts as it had proved elsewhere, organized labor was clearly on the defensive. "We were scared when it was announced that they had enough signatures to get on the ballot," says Paul L'Heureux, a Salem electrician. Winning an uphill electoral battle involved a substantial commitment of resources and a unified sense of purpose that seemed beyond the labor community.

If any wing of the House of Labor was an unlikely candidate to unite disparate sectors of the work force, it was the building trades. While construction unions have long been involved in Massachusetts politics, they are also noted for their history of internal squabbling among the trades and for a "go-it-alone" attitude in relation to the rest of the labor movement. "We're a peculiar breed," jokes Leo Purcell, president of the Massachusetts Building Trades Council. "It often seems like we're in a world of our own."

Construction workers do tend to think they are different and their work unlike any other occupation. The shared exposure to danger, the terrifying insecurity of the boom-and-bust aspect of the business, and the physically demanding yet skilled nature of the work serve as powerful bonds among craft workers. For those who survive the initial years of adjustment, there is a sense of having entered a club that those on the outside can neither understand nor appreciate.

Those special ties underpin a culture that is a source of great pride to many craft workers. Those same ties also foster an "insider" versus "outsider" mentality that can be a barrier to developing ties to the broader community. In the early stages of the campaign, there was little assurance that the insular building trades had the will or the ability to engage in the kind of bridge-building that wins elections. Nor was it a certainty that potential allies—even within the labor movement—would rally around an issue that was intially understood to have an impact only on construction workers.

Workers in the manufacturing, service, clerical, and public sectors all had to be convinced that the fight to preserve the prevailing wage was their battle. Public employees, in particular, remembered the CLT-sponsored "Proposition $2^1/_2$" referendum of 1980. Exit polls at the time indicated that building trades workers were among the groups that had put the ballot measure over the top. The ensuing decade of shrinking public services and meager wages for teachers, firefighters, and police had left deep scars.

Nancy Mills is the director of the ten-thousand member Service Employees International Union, Local 285, in Boston. In April 1988 she attended a campaign meeting as part of a delegation of unions representing large numbers of low-waged women and minority workers. "I had to be honest. Our members felt as if they'd been ignored, as if they didn't have that much in common with the trades despite being in the same labor movement," she reports. "We had an uphill battle—not to convince them of the rightness of the battle, but of a reason to be motivated."

Outside the labor movement, there were more hurdles to overcome. White-collar employees, small-business owners, professionals, and other voters who have often internalized today's pervasive anti-union political bias needed to know that the prevailing wage law was good public policy. And perhaps most important, barriers had to be broken down between the unions and many minority and women's organizations. The reality of restrictive procedures for union membership had left a legacy of bitterness and a reluctance to support the predominantly white male building trades unions without a commitment in return to equal access to the construction industry work force. "There's no question that we'd been on the wrong side of that issue in the past," comments Tom McIntyre, international vice-president of the Bricklayers Union.

To many, these obstacles appeared insurmountable. "A lot of our people had a defeatist attitude in the beginning," notes Harvey Isakson, business representative of a Sheet Metal Workers local and a regional campaign coordinator. "They didn't think they could stand up, fight, and win."

Less than a year passed between the day representatives of the Fair Wage Committee pulled up in an armored truck filled with signatures at the secretary of state's office and Election Day. During that year a series of unexpected steps were taken to ensure the defeat of Question 2. The development of a sophisticated, high-profile media campaign that confronted the false claims of the tax-cutters; the building of an electoral coalition that included consumers, public employees, senior citizens, and a host of community organizations; the opening of a critically important dialogue between the construction unions and minority and women's organizations; the creation of a grass-roots field organization to carry out an ambitious campaign plan; and the ultimate victory—all add up to a story of an invigorated labor movement and a rare chance for citizens to register a clear statement about fair wages and conditions in the workplace.

The campaign successfully stripped the ABC of its image as a taxpayer advocate and recast the organization as a group of self-interested employers eager to undercut decent pay standards and line their own pockets at taxpayers' expense. Responsible economic studies demonstrated that repeal would produce no tax savings, only diminished purchasing power and a lower standard of living. The coalition strategy ensured that the Committee for Quality of Life could legitimately speak in the name of the larger public good. As a result, over the course of the campaign the terms of the conflict shifted from "concerned taxpayer versus Big Labor" to "community interests versus corporate greed."

The 58–42 outcome on Election Day indicated that the unions' message had been heard. Not only was a supposed tax-savings measure defeated, but the breakdown of the vote demonstrates how clearly class based the issue proved to be. Of the 80 upper-income communities in Massachusetts, 60 voted yes on Question 2; of the 271 low- and moderate-income towns and cities, a resounding 243 voted no.[6] "Massachusetts politics will never be the same," Osborn proclaimed the night of November 8. The outlines of possible shifts in political allegiances based on the campaign remain hazy, but what is clear is that, at least on that day, the working people of Massachusetts spoke in a unified voice.

What is also clear is that, for many of the volunteers at the grass-roots level, the campaign provided an opportunity to put the "movement" back in the labor movement. As neighborhood ambassadors for their cause, they proudly and publicly identified themselves with a tradition of democratic and activist unionism. They also learned something about themselves. "Until this campaign," marveled Luis Burgos, a forty-one-year-old operating engineer who had never been particularly active in his union or community, "I didn't think I had the talent to talk to people about an issue I believed in."

2 | The Prevailing Wage

The debate over prevailing wage laws is not easy to untangle from the general question of unionism in construction. Opponents of the laws describe them as outdated and irrelevant to current conditions in the industry. While granting that the original legislation may have been "useful," they claim that continuation of the system only ensures that "organized labor get[s] free rides on the gravy train."[1] Construction union officials, on the other hand, argue that the laws are as relevant today as they ever were, serving to protect community wage standards at a particularly volatile time in the industry's history. Both sides agree that much more is at stake than a single piece of legislation. The very nature of the work in the building trades appears to be tied to the success or failure of campaigns to repeal prevailing wage statutes.

Given the heat of the battle, it is ironic that the originators of prevailing wage legislation were as much government and business reformers as labor advocates. Most government officials continue to view the laws as essentially public policy measures. For example, a 1988 report from the U.S. House Committee on Education and Labor describes the Davis-Bacon Act "as important today as it was" when originally passed. The law exists, the report continues, "not only to promote both public safety and welfare but also to safeguard taxpayers from the predatory practices of unscrupulous contractors and the unwitting damage caused by unskilled workers."[2] In fact, the original motivation for these laws had far less to do with questions of collective bargaining than with the peculiarities of the construction business.

Construction has always been and still is the "Wild West" of American industry. Individual firms enter and leave the industry constantly. In 1982 (the year of the Census Bureau's most recent survey) there were 1.4 million construction establishments in the United States; more than nine hundred thousand carried out their work with no employees.[3] These "mom-and-pop" builders pose no threat to the

Bechtels, Fluor Daniels, Turners, and other giants who dominate construction, but their very existence demonstrates that there is still a niche for small outfits that operate with little more capital than leased equipment, pickup truck, wheelbarrow, and a set of tools.

The persistence of large numbers of local and regional contractors and subcontractors along with a whole set of related but often antagonistic players—architect, banker, developer, engineer, and so on—combine to create an industry without a clearly defined center. There are no giant corporations whose very size and associated clout have traditionally set standards for business practices and industrial relations that others either accept or fight against. Ironically, it has been the unions in construction that have provided much of the industry's limited stability by initiating labor relations standards through collective bargaining, apprenticeship programs, and hiring halls.

The chaos of construction has always posed a problem for government agencies. With so many employers and so few universally accepted business procedures in the construction industry, federal, state, and local bodies have written reams of regulations in order to protect taxpayer investment in public building programs. In particular, the issue of wage levels has long been a subject of scrutiny.

Unlike procedures in the private sector, public agencies are generally required to award construction projects to the lowest bidder. With expenses such as materials and financing fixed by outside forces, contractors can manipulate only one factor in their estimates—labor costs. A system that rewards the lowest bidder without setting pay guidelines inevitably favors those employers who are willing to slash wages deeper than the competition. Fly-by-night builders with a low-paid, unskilled, casual work force and a minimal commitment to product quality are therefore the likely winners.

It was precisely this dilemma that the prevailing wage laws were meant to resolve. In 1891 Kansas adopted a law requiring that construction workers employed by or on behalf of the state be paid "not less than the current rate of per diem wages in the locality where the work is performed."[4] Kansas was the first of forty-one states that ultimately chose this form of legislation in order to create a level playing field for all bidders on public construction. With wages taken out of competition, state agencies could be more confident that low bids would reflect managerial efficiency rather than unscrupulous labor practices.

In 1914 Massachusetts became the sixth state to enact a prevailing wage law. The Board of Labor and Industries was charged with administration of the new law, and the scale was defined as "not less than the customary and prevailing rate of wages for a day's work in the same trade or occupation." In 1935 the statute was modified to allow "collective agreements or understandings between organized labor and employers" to be the basis of the Board of Labor and Industries' determinations.[5]

Opponents of prevailing wage legislation regularly claim that many of the state laws and, in particular, the federal Davis-Bacon Act were products of a Depression and/or New Deal era mentality that is no longer relevant. The legislative history suggests otherwise. In 1927 (a year of prosperity in the building industry) Congressman Robert Bacon (R–N.Y.), a banker from Long Island, first introduced the measure at the national level. Recounting the problems created in his congressional district by the arrival of a thousand out-of-state workers, paid low wages and housed in temporary shacks, Bacon urged the government "to comply with the local standards of wages and labor prevailing in the locality where the building construction is to take place."[6] Bacon and others feared that publicly sponsored cutthroat bidding by itinerant contractors would mushroom under the extensive ten-year building program authorized by Congress in 1926.

Bacon refiled his legislation in 1928. In a memorandum of support, Commissioner of Labor Statistics Ethelbert Stewart wrote: "The essence of the thing as I see it is: Is the Government willing for the sake of the lowest bidder to break down all labor standards and have its work done by the cheapest labor that can be secured and shipped from State to State?"[7] In 1931 the bill (now cosponsored by James Davis, a Republican senator from Pennsylvania) was adopted without opposition by both the House and Senate and signed into law by President Herbert Hoover.

Legislators addressed a variety of technical problems over the next four years. In 1935 a comprehensive Davis-Bacon amendment was passed that set the terms for federal policy on public construction for the next five decades. Davis-Bacon continued to enjoy bipartisan endorsements in Congress and equal measures of support from both industry and labor. The law was sufficiently widely accepted to serve as a model for federal legislation governing service contracts as well as additional prevailing wage measures at the state level.

The challenge to the prevailing wage laws is not an indication of their failure to stabilize an unstable industry. Instead, it reflects a recent and fundamental shift in philosophy on the part of key actors in and around the construction business. The rules of the game have changed dramatically in the past twenty years. In 1969 union construction workers were responsible for 80 percent of all construction activity in the United States. Today the figure is closer to 35 percent. That is the backdrop for the intense pressure on prevailing wage legislation. The basic structure of construction is unchanged. The overall need for stability and a level playing field is as great as ever. What has changed is the economic and political influence of the non-union sector and its desire to reframe the political agenda of the industry.

The roots of this shift can be found in the inflationary climate of the late 1960s. Prices spiraled in the war-driven American economy, and the building industry was no exception. Rising costs of materials and labor shortages jacked up the price of construction. Many corporate leaders, management consultants, policymakers, and business journalists pinned the blame for the price increases on construction workers and their labor organizations. A 1968 *Fortune* article accused the "most powerful oligopoly in the American economy," that is, the building trades unions, of being responsible for the "stranglehold in construction."[8] A number of business leaders began to confer in public gatherings and private meetings in order to develop a strategy to control costs and blunt union leverage. The U.S. Chamber of Commerce, the National Association of Manufacturers, and a newly formed organization called the Construction Users Anti-Inflation Roundtable, all weighed in with recommendations. Founded in 1969 by the former chairman of United States Steel, Roger Blough, the Roundtable included on its original policy committee the chief executive officers of General Motors, General Electric, Standard Oil, Union Carbide, AT&T, and Kennecott Copper. Three years later the Roundtable merged with the Labor Law Study Group, an association of anti-union labor relations executives and corporate attorneys, to form the Business Roundtable.

The Roundtable has gone on to become one of the leading voices of the business community, representing some two hundred of the nation's top CEOs. They are, in the words of former representative Wright Patman of Texas, the "fattest of the fat cats."[9] Yet while many people are familiar with the fabled influence of the Roundtable, few realize that the organization emerged from a corporate effort to reshape the construction industry in its own image. In one of its first publications, the Roundtable sternly lectured building contractors on their inability to prevent unions from "usurp[ing] the employer role normally reserved to management in other industries." In the lengthy and widely distributed report, the CEOs spelled out a series of very specific steps to "restore the control that employers traditionally exercise."[10]

According to the Roundtable and its allies, the key to limiting union power was to increase the role of the non-union sector in construction. Large employers, such as Du Pont and Dow Chemical, began to exclude union contractors from their bid lists as they consciously set out to sponsor and nurture non-union builders. At a 1968 conference in Texas of two hundred industrial owners and building contractors, one of the principal speakers urged insurance companies and banks not to use their funds in any way that might support the union sector. These targeted financing policies, he explained, were "as simple as the banker's right to grant or reject a loan based on no other reason than that he doesn't like on which side of your head you parted your hair."[11]

Corporate sponsorship of the non-union sector

soon bore fruit. By 1972 the Associated Builders and Contractors, once a marginal association of a handful of residential and small-scale commercial builders, had quickly grown to a membership of forty-six hundred, including seventeen of the nation's four hundred top contractors. Outside some major urban centers, non-union contractors rose to positions of prominence throughout the country in the following decade. Open-shop firms represented 29 percent of the top four hundred list by 1984. Furthermore, eight of the nation's top ten contractors that year were "double-breasted," that is, operating with both union and non-union divisions.[12]

The Roundtable succeeded beyond its wildest dreams, in part because of its foresight, persistence, and enormous economic clout, and in part because of the coincidence in the mid-1970s of a severely depressed building industry that rewarded contractors with low labor costs. Furthermore, the Roundtable succeeded in sponsoring a breed of builders who reflected corporate values. ABC members are not only against unionism; they are proponents of the so-called merit-shop philosophy. Union construction is a relatively collective and egalitarian method of production in which the product reflects the ability and experience of the individual craft workers. Open-shop building is more highly specialized and organized on a hierarchical basis. Control is, as the Roundtable reports demanded, firmly in the hands of the employer.

The difference between the union and the non-union sectors cannot be measured solely on the basis of wages. There is a fundamental ideological conflict between the ABC's corporate, individualistic world view and the more collective production system that operates on union construction sites. Except for apprentices, union workers in each trade are paid uniform wages and expected to perform similar tasks with a high degree of competence over a lifetime of skilled work. In the non-union arena, a handful of well-paid, qualified skilled workers (often trained in union programs) oversee dozens of young, inexperienced, low-paid workers with a short-term commitment to the industry. The non-union and union sectors represent two different worlds and two different cultures: The former emphasizes competitive individualism; the latter draws on traditions of cooperation and solidarity. The difference in pay scales mirrors these opposing attitudes. "Personally, I could never be in a union," comments Stephen Tocco, former executive vice-president of the Massachusetts ABC, "because I think I'm better than the guy next to me. And I want to get paid more for it."[13]

3 | Clouds on the Horizon

In their early strategy sessions on the construction industry, the Business Roundtable set four key goals: boosting the fortunes of the open-shop sector, intervening in collective bargaining through local "user" (that is, large employer) groups, funding anti-union research and litigation, and repealing the Davis-Bacon Act. Roundtable members were politically sophisticated enough to recognize that, even with their influence, a law with a history of such broad support could not be eliminated overnight. Therefore, they outlined a long-range plan to undermine the consensus in support of the Davis-Bacon Act.

The first step was to develop credibility for the open-shop movement. To accomplish this goal, the Roundtable and several construction employer associations financially supported much of the work of researchers Herbert Northrup and Armand Thieblot of the Wharton School of Finance at the University of Pennsylvania. Northrup's *Open Shop Construction*, published in 1975, became the first scholarly account of the development of the non-union sector. Similarly, Thieblot's *Davis-Bacon Act* was played up as an academic critique of the federal legislation. Their books, along with articles by friendly journalists, were the building blocks of a new consensus, one that openly sided with anti-union forces and challenged the rationale for the Davis-Bacon law.

During 1975 the Roundtable purchased more than one hundred pages of advertising space in *Reader's Digest*, at a cost of $1.2 million, to run a series called "Our Economic System: You Make It Work." The piece in the April issue called for the repeal of Davis-Bacon. Four years later, the federal government's General Accounting Office (GAO) issued an influential report titled *The Davis-Bacon Act Should Be Repealed*. The years of carefully orchestrated research, publicity, and promotion paid off. The *New York Times*, the *Wall Street Journal*, the *Washington Post*, and other widely read publications began to echo the call for repeal. "We no longer have to sell the fact that Davis-Bacon is inflationary," announced a pleased ABC spokesman in 1978. "From our standpoint, if the political climate is ever going to be ripe, it is now."[1]

By this time, the ABC had sufficient members, resources, and staff to emerge from under the Roundtable's protective wing. In 1979 it unveiled a two-pronged national legislative strategy. On the one hand, the ABC called for elimination of Davis-Bacon. If, however, outright repeal was unattainable, it was prepared to chip away at the edges of the law through a variety of amendments that would either raise the threshold of jobs covered by the act or exempt projects in military construction, housing programs, airport aid, mass transit, and other federal programs.

The movement in the Senate to repeal Davis-Bacon was initiated by Orrin Hatch (R–Utah) and backed by supporting statements from the National Association of Manufacturers, U.S. Chamber of Commerce, and Associated General Contractors, in addition to the Roundtable and ABC. The assault on Davis-Bacon was one of the early legislative shots fired by the forces coalescing in the New Right that would take Ronald Reagan to the White House two years later. At the same time efforts to appeal or weaken state prevailing wage laws were underway. "Thirty-nine states have Davis-Bacon legislation, and thirty-one states are attempting to recall that legislation," said Robert Georgine, president of the national Building and Construction Trades Department (BCTD) of the AFL-CIO. "If that's not a concerted effort, I don't know what is."[2]

Reports of a $500,000 ABC war chest circulated as the opposition to Davis-Bacon intensified. The Florida and Alabama legislatures repealed their prevailing wage laws in 1979. Utah's legislation fell two years later. Nonetheless, opponents of Davis-Bacon continued to be unable to convince a majority in Congress. Hatch, Senator Jake Garn (R–Utah), and other ABC supporters filed bills each legislative session, but to no avail. The failure to win congressional approval prompted ABC strategists to shift their emphasis from the legislative to the executive branch. While President Reagan personally released either noncommittal or pro–Davis-Bacon statements, other members of his administration were outspoken allies of the opposition.

In 1982 Secretary of Labor Raymond Donovan unexpectedly issued a set of regulations transforming the administration of the law. An angry Lane Kirkland, president of the AFL-CIO, charged that Donovan's action amounted to a "back door attempt to nullify the law."[3] The new regulations, while technical in nature, were designed to hamper standard operating procedures in the union sector and to support non-union methods of operation. For example, the Donovan rules expanded the role of "helpers," a category of semiskilled workers common on non-union projects and foreign to the traditional apprentice–journeyman system in union construction. In addition, the elimination of the so-called 30 percent rule along with other changes ensured that union wage standards would become increasingly irrelevant in determining the prevailing rate on federal jobs.

In a memo to Vice-President George Bush, Donovan suggested that his rulings "should be very well received by contractor groups" but indicated that the unions affected "may react unfavorably." His prediction was accurate. Speaking for the U.S. Chamber of Commerce, G. John Tysse pronounced himself "pleasantly surprised." ABC President John Fielder called the Labor Department's announcement "the most positive step we've seen on the issue in a long time." *Builder and Contractor*, the ABC's national magazine, proclaimed Donovan the "Construction Man of the Year" for 1983. Pat Alibrandi, a Massachusetts electrical contractor and Fielder's successor as ABC president, summarized the new relationship with the Reagan administration: "Under previous administrations, ABC was sometimes a less than welcome visitor to the corridors of the Labor Department. But with Secretary Donovan, ABC is more than just a welcomed guest; we are frequently called upon for advice and assistance at all levels within the Department."[4]

The AFL-CIO Executive Council, on the other hand, reported that it was "shocked and angered" and vowed to fight the regulations. In June 1982 the BCTD and the AFL-CIO asked a federal court to intervene to prevent the Labor Department's alteration of Davis-Bacon "by administrative fiat." After three years of protracted litigation, an appeals court overruled some provisions but allowed the bulk of Donovan's rulings to stand. In particular, the court supported the new wage-determination system as well as the employment of helpers in areas where that job classification prevailed.[5]

Supporters and opponents of Davis-Bacon in Congress continue to debate the issue, but divisions remain sufficiently deep to block the passage of any related legislation. For now, the Donovan rulings represent the ABC's clearest victory at the national level. The Davis-Bacon Act never mandated that local prevailing rates had to correspond to union scales—in fact, a 1978 Department of Labor study revealed that only 43 percent of all federally determined local wages surveyed corresponded to the union rate. But the extension of the open shop into large-scale construction and the revised Labor Department regulations have combined to accomplish one of the ABC's most important goals. With the exception of union strongholds, the collective-bargaining system in construction has increasingly little to do with the contents of workers' pay envelopes on federally funded projects.

The early reports advocating repeal of Davis-Bacon all stressed the inflationary character of the law. This emphasis rested less on reasoned economic arguments than on the Roundtable's desire to reverse a late 1960s national trend in which wages were rising faster than profits. Clearly, corporate leaders could not openly acknowledge their desire for profit making at the expense of an improved standard of living for working people. Therefore, an argument blaming inflation on wage increases had to be developed. Since construction wages were on the rise, opponents of Davis-Bacon promoted the following quick, if flawed, chain of logic: The overall economic climate is inflationary; union construction wages are rising; prevailing wage rates are based on union scales; rising union rates will increase costs on public projects covered by prevailing wage statutes; increased costs on public projects require additional federal funds; excessive federal spending overheats the economy; therefore, the Davis-Bacon Act is inflationary.

The problem with this neat package was that it had little to do with reality. Many of the early studies were strictly advocacy pieces with little factual evidence. Careful readings of the Roundtable reports, for example, revealed that their underlying interest was additional managerial control in the industry rather than the reform of difficult economic conditions. The lengthy 1979 General Accounting Office (GAO) report was, therefore, a godsend. It loudly and unequivocally called for repeal and had the advantage of a seal of approval from a presumably impartial government agency.

Once again, appearances proved to be deceiving. The GAO's recommendations were quickly rejected by the Labor Department, the Department of Housing and Urban Development, and the Office of Management and Budget. Close examinations of the report demonstrated that it was based on inadequate information. For example, the claim that the legislation was inflationary rested on a sample of thirty cases out of a total of eighteen thousand wage determinations. For those readers who were willing to plow through the first hundred pages, the report contained an important admission: "We recognize that our sample size was insufficient for projecting the results to the universe of construction costs during the year with any statistical validity." Unfortunately, that warning did not keep the report's authors from describing Davis-Bacon as "the most inflationary piece of legislation in America today."[6]

Criticisms of ABC arguments were drowned in a sea of well-financed public relations. Despite the limited evidence, the link between inflation and prevailing wage laws had been established in the public eye by a decade of endlessly repeated claims. As the 1970s wore on, however, the problem of inflation became less acute in the American economy. Furthermore, the severe building slump was rewriting industry assumptions. The wage hikes of the 1960s were quickly overtaken by pay cuts or freezes. Blaming overpaid construction workers for inflation was considerably less convincing when those same workers were struggling with a 22 percent unemployment rate and a declining standard of living.

As a result, ABC leaders cast about for a new political hook to hang their hats on. If the charge of inflationary wage behavior held less water, perhaps the emerging "taxpayers' revolt" movement could be tied in with an attack on the publicly supported prevailing wage. The battle to enact Proposition 13 in California had demonstrated that an appeal to the taxpayer as the aggrieved "little guy" had tremendous political potential. Tapping into that anti–big government and pro-pocketbook sentiment could propel the ABC to new political heights.

The ABC chose to try out its new approach at the state level, just as the Proposition 13 organizers had done. In Utah, for example, local ABC leaders started to build a coalition of city, town, and county officials to support a state legislative campaign. The ABC hoped that these local officials would lobby state officeholders on behalf of their communities. In addition, elected community leaders were seen as more effective advocates with the media than self-interested contractors might be. The Utah ABC outlined its overall strategy in a letter to other state ABC chapters in 1978: "It was our hope that the major argument in favor of repeal could be based on tax savings and unnecessary government spending, rather than a union versus non-union argument."[7] The strategy succeeded. Repeal of Utah's prevailing wage law occurred three years later.

If non-union builders in Utah opened the discussion of a new comprehensive strategy, Massachusetts contractors refined it. Under the leadership of Stephen Tocco, the Massachusetts/Rhode Island ABC emerged in the 1980s as the organization's flagship chapter in terms of political sophistication. By 1985 the chapter had more than 670 members, making it the ABC's single largest branch. Its influence even exceeded its size. In 1987 the national ABC awarded half of its annual President's Awards to the Massachusetts/Rhode Island chapter for its legislative work, publications, and management education.

Recognition of the chapter's accomplishments rested almost exclusively on its unceasing efforts to eliminate the Massachusetts prevailing wage law. Tocco borrowed the "populist" coalition-building tactics proposed in Utah to position himself and his organization as contenders on the state political scene. While the membership of the ABC simply sought political initiatives that would increase their business opportunities, Tocco shrewdly recognized that success hinged on shoving blatant contractor interests to the side while pushing the image of general public concern into the foreground.

Tocco became a regular guest on radio talk shows and a frequent contributor to the op-ed section of the state's newspapers. He regularly painted himself as the underdog David fighting the "Big Labor" Goliaths, as the political outsider operating in a state where unions had a long-standing "sweetheart deal" with the legislature. He complained that craven politicians feared bucking organized labor and, as a result, refused to consider seriously the merits of arguments against the prevailing wage law.

In a state where unionism is not always a dirty

word, Tocco was careful not to go too far. "I don't see this as a union battle," he claimed. "I see it as a government procurement problem." Tocco would always point out that he was not opposed to unions per se, just union abuses. In fact, in a 1983 column in the *Boston Globe*, he favorably compared the wisdom of the United Auto Workers (UAW) officials who endorsed labor–management cooperation with the arrogance of power-hungry and corrupt building trades union officials who "present a mirror image of the Robber Barons unions fought so courageously and righteously many years ago." Tocco and other ABC members seized on the popular impression that modern unions function with a vast gulf between leadership and membership. "While they have had the power to block [prevailing wage repeal] on Beacon Hill," argued ABC lobbyist Roger Donoghue, "they no longer have the clout on the streets."[8]

The ABC also drew on other popular political images. Virtually every mention of the prevailing wage laws was preceded by the words *outdated* or *archaic* in an effort to appeal to the trendy, young, upwardly mobile voter who dominated the 1980s cultural and advertising scene. ABC supporter Representative Stephen Doran described the law as "byzantine" and motivated by economic conditions that "no longer exist." Doran, described by Massachusetts AFL-CIO President Arthur Osborn as "the boy representative from Lexington who never had dirt under his fingernails," represented a community that ranks eleventh in the state in per capita income. "Yuppies," argued

Roger Donoghue, referring to this constituency, "are generally not big labor supporters like their parents were."[9]

While upscale voters and the business community may have been the ABC's natural constituency, Tocco consistently claimed to speak on behalf of a broader cross section of the population. The trade unions, he insisted, were the isolated special interest. Donning the garb of the silent majority, he proclaimed: "The voice of the people is often drowned out by the shouts of special interest groups. . . . Let the people's voice be heard!" The ABC-sponsored coalition, he continued, "is a grass roots organization which represents the will of the people."[10]

Tocco went so far as to imply that he was really a social reformer and not the agent of an employers' organization seeking to protect and extend its own interests. In his eyes, the prevailing wage law was the scourge of progress, standing in the way of affordable housing, adequate schools, well-maintained roads and bridges, and solutions to prison overcrowding and the plight of the homeless. "We have some tough choices to make, as a society," Tocco told an interviewer. "Whether we decide we want to continue to build affordable housing for elderly or homeless or anybody—or do we want to hold onto sacred cows that are outdated, extremely expensive and have a direct impact on those other needs."[11]

Perhaps most cynically, Tocco periodically tried on the mantle of a champion of women and minorities. Never at a loss to find fault with the prevailing wage law, he once wrote that "this outdated statute . . . discriminates against open shop contractors, females, and minorities." Suggesting that non-union builders embodied the spirit of opportunity, Tocco capitalized on the building trades unions' reputations as white male institutions with exclusionary histories. What Tocco always failed to mention was open-shop employers' own dismal track record on access. A comparison of ABC-sponsored training programs and union apprenticeship programs in 1988, for example, indicates that more than twice as many women and nearly four times as many African-Americans, Hispanics, and other minorities participated in the union programs. The entire industry, union and non-union, has failed to come to grips with the issue of affirmative action but the open-shop sector lags farther behind.[12]

Legitimate or not, the content of the ABC road show was in place. All that remained was to start the tryouts. Legislative supporters introduced bills in 1979 and 1981, but the first serious effort began in 1982. At the end of that year, the ABC put together a series of strategy meetings. Organizations in attendance included Citizens for Limited Taxation, the Massachusetts High Technology Council, the Smaller Business Association of New England, local Chambers of Commerce, the Massachusetts Taxpayers Foundation, and the Massachusetts Municipal Association. With the exception of the MMA, this coalition pops up under a variety of guises and names on virtually every political issue that affects the state's business community.

The December 29 meeting produced decisions that would guide ABC strategy for the next six years. Participants in the strategy sessions voted to drop the name originally chosen for their organization, the Prevailing Wage Coalition, in favor of the more generic Committee for Local Option on Contracts (CLOC). The group issued a call for a list of "horror stories" to dramatize the high cost of the law. Coalition members agreed to "argue the issues on economic terms and not as a labor/management dispute." Finally, and most interesting, the participants stressed that a "major effort should be made to attract a municipal union for support." Flush from the success of Proposition $2^1/_2$, the coalition believed it could sow further dissension in the ranks of organized labor and pit building trades workers against state and municipal employees, who relied on shrinking public funds.[13]

In February 1983 Democratic state representatives Al Minahan, Stephen Doran, and Tom Vallely filed a bill that would allow cities and towns the "local option" of waiving the state prevailing wage law on projects in their communities. Despite a fairly successful media campaign, the legislation lost in the House by a vote of 128 to 19. Undaunted, the ABC pressed on. Over the next two years, their State House allies introduced a series of scattershot measures related to the prevailing wage issue. Passage of all these bills would have set the prevailing wage at 80 percent of the union rate, introduced a classification of helpers payable at twice the minimum wage, increased the ratio of apprentices to journeymen, and restricted coverage of the law to projects that exceeded $250,000.

Its persistent activity drew attention to the ABC and its concerns but failed to gain significant additional support in the legislature. As early as 1983, alternative strategies were mapped out. In a meeting that year, CLOC members decided they would travel the referendum route if legislative success appeared unreachable. Although they continued to advocate their legislation, ABC leaders gradually shifted gears over the next two years. Hinting that their future pointed toward a ballot question, the organization's spokesmen began to prepare their membership for this new direction. ABC publications regularly referred to the success of Proposition $2\frac{1}{2}$ and suggested that the ballot route was a transferable strategy, one in which "citizens could take state government by the throat."[14]

In 1985 the ABC shed the cloak of the CLOC and adopted a new cover, the Taxpayers Initiative for Municipal Efficiency. TIME was composed of the same cast of characters as the CLOC, but its new name more clearly linked it to the tax-cutting movement. Former Republican gubernatorial candidate Greg Hyatt was hired to spearhead the signature drive, officially launched on September 18. The nine-week effort fell short. TIME needed 61,000 signatures to get on the ballot and collected only 56,000.

The five-thousand-name shortfall both frustrated and encouraged ABC organizers. While they had failed to get their proposal on the ballot, they had come tantalizingly close in spite of limited expertise and an inexperienced campaign organization, not to mention Hyatt's bizarre performance as campaign manager, which undermined staff morale. Tocco later fired Hyatt, saying he was "drunk in his office, homeless, slept overnight in the office, would run around the office without any clothes on and would talk into the telephone without anyone on the other end."[15] Given the unusual circumstances, most TIME staffers concluded that a second go-round with improved leadership and training would undoubtedly produce enough signatures. The ABC Board of Directors was sufficiently persuaded to fund a continuing full-time political campaign.

Two years later, the ABC pulled yet another name out of the hat. TIME gave way to the Fair Wage Committee, which represented the same set of organizations that had endorsed the ABC's two previous incarnations. The new committee's fortunes looked brighter in the context of a changing political environment. The practice of politics-through-referendum was becoming more widely established. A corps of political consultants quickly recognized the potential new market and advertised their services to interested groups. Their advice included the recommendation that signature gatherers be paid workers, not volunteers, a notion that had withstood the scrutiny of state election laws.

Accordingly, the Fair Wage Committee modified its campaign strategy. Staff salaries were boosted by 50 percent. Led by Tocco and lobbyist Martin Burke, the campaign focused on four counties (Worcester, Middlesex, Plymouth, and Essex) rather than randomly targeting the entire state. And in an important shift, the signature gatherers in 1987 were paid according to the number of names collected. The message, however, remained constant: Downplay the wage issue and focus on taxes. "They'd say whatever anyone wanted to hear when they were getting the names," remembers Michael Molinari of the State Council of Carpenters. "In the malls, they'd say, 'Are you interested in a tax cut?' In the elderly housing complexes, they'd ask, 'Wouldn't you like a few extra units?'"

On December 2 the Fair Wage Committee turned in more than enough signatures to win a spot on the ballot. The tide seemed to be running in the ABC's direction. In a statement issued to the press, Tocco confidently predicted that the people of Massachusetts "will vote overwhelmingly [to repeal] the Prevailing Wage Law in November 1988."[16] Many trade unionists reluctantly agreed with Tocco's assessment. "Once the signatures were in, I assumed the public would oppose us," recalls Martin Ploof, a

Carpenters Union official. "They had the momentum and it was unclear to me if the building trades unions could overcome past internal animosities to work together."

4 | Looking for Answers

The rapid rise of the open shop caught most union leaders off guard. The post–World War II prosperity in construction ushered in an extended period of relative comfort and an accompanying sense of complacency. By and large, work was plentiful, wages were rising, new benefits accompanied each contract, and the local unions were running on automatic pilot. The non-union builders who worked on the periphery of the industry in the 1950s and 1960s appeared to represent little threat.

An occasional voice challenged the prevailing serenity. In 1968—at a time when union work accounted for 80 percent of all construction—Carpenters Union organizer Abe Saul, for one, warned members of his craft in Massachusetts: "The trades are too busy squabbling with one another, too busy looking for power within the Building Trades Council to concentrate on the common enemy, the 'scab' contractor, and he has taken advantage of it."[1] Other unionists shared these fears, but their warnings were largely cries in the wilderness.

The developments of the 1970s destroyed the reigning calm. High unemployment, corporate sponsorship of non-union contractors, and the emergence of a political climate openly hostile to labor all punctured the union balloon. The open-shop share of the construction market increased dramatically in Massachusetts, as it did across the country. Reliable figures are few and far between, but most observers agree that non-union builders now collect over half of the total construction dollars in the state. An exhaustive study by Stephen Krasner indicates that the union share of electrical work in the greater Boston area slid from 81 percent in 1971 to 54 percent in 1985.[2] The general outline for all trades today is similar. Downtown Boston construction is still monopolized by union firms, and a simple majority of the work in the greater Boston area is union-built, but outside the city the open shop dominates. In some areas as little as one-third of construction work is done by unionized workers.

The union leadership was also caught by surprise

by political developments. Ten years of Business Roundtable strategy sessions and ABC growth had been monitored by the Building and Construction Trades Department at the national level, but most local unions were too preoccupied with the day-to-day crises of unemployment and declining market share to stand back and look at national trends. Some of the early prevailing wage repeal bills, particularly in the Sunbelt states, encountered little organized resistance in the state legislatures.

In Massachusetts the presence of a heavily Democratic legislature ensured that repeal efforts would not slide through. The initial ABC ventures were defeated by lopsided votes, providing the building trades unions an opportunity to catch their collective breath and prepare counterstrategies. Still, the seeming security provided by a sympathetic legislature offered little comfort. The issue was new to Massachusetts, and the ABC was just beginning to flex its muscles. To the extent that the prevailing wage law was successfully linked to tax-cutting initiatives, politicians' convictions could easily waver. Tocco, after all, had used the legislative setbacks to enhance his underdog image in the media. The issue might not have appeared to have much of a future at the State House, but it was alive and well in the newspapers and on the airwaves.

The threat to wages and living standards posed by repeal of the prevailing wage law was recognized early on by some of those most immediately affected. In March 1983 unemployed construction workers picketed outside the houses of two of the sponsors of the local-option legislation. One month later, hundreds of union members walked off their downtown job sites to attend public hearings on the bill at the State House. In an open letter to his state representative published in the local newspaper, Mike Novelli of Wakefield asked: "Do you really believe that I am a threat to the economics of this state?" Novelli suggested that Representative Minahan consider the impact of other players in the construction game, such as bankers, suppliers, contractors, and land developers. In a refrain that would be heard over and over again five years later, Novelli concluded: "There are a lot of problems in our district, in this state and in this country. As an unemployed construction worker, I fail to see how they can be solved by cutting my wages."[3]

As long as the ABC restricted its activity to the legislature, union officials could limit their efforts to lobbying legislators and mobilizing members to attend the annual public hearings in Gardner Auditorium at the State House. In 1985 more than six hundred construction workers packed the hall to hear testimony that, according to the *Boston Globe*, "was frequently interrupted by bursts of cheers for the bills' opponents or boos, hisses and heckling for proponents."[4] Once the forum changed to a ballot initiative, however, a new strategy was in order.

In late summer 1985 a group of labor leaders, headed by Arthur Osborn and Massachusetts Building Trades Council President Tom Evers, drew up a plan to counter TIME's signature drive. They proposed the formation of the Massachusetts Coalition for Quality Construction, a steering committee to represent consumers, senior citizens, minorities, women, academics, students, and religious organizations on the issue of the prevailing wage law. The coalition never really left the planning stages, but the group did map out a strategy to keep down the number of signatures that TIME could gather.

The center of the operation was a hotline installed in the state AFL-CIO office and coordinated by AFL-CIO staffer Richard Rogers. The hotline number was distributed to all building trades unions, other labor unions, and groups identified as potential members of the coalition. The hotline was intended to monitor and deter ABC signature collectors. Anyone who saw a volunteer circulating the TIME petitions was instructed to call the state AFL-CIO. Rogers reported the activity to Evers, who, in turn, notified the particular construction union business agent responsible for that geographical area on that particular day. The business agent then dispatched someone to stand alongside the ABC operative, hand out fliers headed "Don't Sign Away *Our* Future," and urge voters not to sign.

Each local union in the building trades was on call at various times and locations on a rotating basis. Assistance also came from the United Food and Commercial Workers, the International Ladies Garment Workers, and the United Auto Workers, whose members were employed in some of the stores, shopping centers, and malls frequented by the signature collectors. In the last few weeks of the drive, the hotline was well-enough organized to concern ABC leaders. Tocco described the union reaction as "very aggressive" and charged the unions with harassment. When pressed by reporters to define harassment, Tocco responded vaguely. One TIME volunteer indignantly complained about a bricklayer who told shoppers that "we were union busters trying to cut his wages."[5]

"We are pleased that they failed," John Davoren, legislative director of the Massachusetts Building Trades Council, reported at the time. "There was no groundswell of support for ABC's position." But most union officials recognized that they were not out of the woods. Both sides assumed that 1985 was a trial run for a more ambitious attempt. Two years later the ABC's Board of Directors voted to create the Fair Wage Committee and authorized yet another assault on the prevailing wage. Standing in front of the State House on September 15, 1987, as part of a series of statewide campaign kickoff press conferences, Stephen Tocco announced: "It is our intention, having been shut out of the legislative process completely on this issue, to take it to the people."[6]

The Fair Wage Committee filed five separate initiative petitions with the state attorney general's office on August 5. Each one was a slight variation on the basic theme, a mix-and-match combination of issues piggybacked on top of prevailing wage repeal.

On the Friday before Labor Day, Osborn, along with building trades leaders Tom McIntyre, Joe Nigro, and Charles Raso, met with Attorney General James Shannon. As representatives of the Boston Building Trades Council, Nigro and Raso had already requested an injunction against the Fair Wage Committee on the grounds that the petitions did not satisfy the legal requirement of "relatedness of multiple subjects." On September 11 Shannon threw out three of the ABC petitions that contained language regarding apprentice ratios and new wage formulas. He did, however, allow the remaining two, narrower versions, thus opening the path for a spot on the ballot.

Once again, the construction unions cranked their machinery into motion. Under Evers's direction, building trades councils across the state set up another battery of regional hotlines. On the North Shore, for example, the Salem office of the International Brotherhood of Electrical Workers (IBEW) served as the central clearinghouse. During the day business agents from the IBEW or the Plumbers Union monitored calls. At night the phone calls were sometimes transferred to other union offices or to the homes of various officers. The area covered by the hotlines was broken down into smaller units, as each of the trades took responsibility for different towns.

The Pioneer Valley Building Trades Council instituted a similar system. Each of the three counties in the valley was divided into seven regions. A building trades business agent was appointed to coordinate each of the twenty-one areas on a seven-day-a-week, twelve-hour-a-day basis. The twenty-one captains were handed lists of union members in their geographical jurisdictions, and time slots were assigned to rank-and-file volunteers so that no one had more than three half-day obligations.

In Boston the hotline was located at the IBEW's Freeport Hall. IBEW Local 103's staff answered the phones during the day, and other unions picked up the slack at night. In all of the areas, the response system was similar. "We had contacts in each town," says Russell Sheehan, business manager of IBEW 103. "A call would come in saying there was someone at, say, a mall in Dedham, and we'd dispatch people with fliers." The union member would stand next to the Fair Wage Committee's campaigner and urge voters not to sign the petition.

Harvey Isakson was working at his desk in the Sheet Metal Workers office the day John Jones, national president of the ABC, came to Worcester to open the campaign. "I looked out the window and saw him down on the Common. I went to my car, got some pamphlets, and told the people there that the petition would only hurt working people's wages. The ABC folks left soon after." Marty Ploof recalls a similar encounter at a church bingo session. "Three people from [ABC contractor] Plumb House were asking the senior citizens if they wanted lower taxes. Once people knew the real issue, they wouldn't sign.

In fact, once the parish priest knew what it was about, he wouldn't give them the space again."

The hotline volunteers did dissuade many people from signing, enough so that the Fair Wage Committee sought an injunction requiring union workers to stay 150 feet away from the signature gatherers. In its suit the Fair Wage Committee described union activity as "organized and pervasive" and charged that incidents of "loud and boisterous behavior" were "disrupting the signature gathering." Affidavits accompanying the suit failed to detail any serious instances of intimidation. When pressed on this point, Tocco attributed the lack of evidence to fear of retaliation. On October 19 Superior Court Judge Guy Volterra quickly dismissed the case.[7]

The ABC anticipated the union hotlines in 1987. Rather than lose arguments with union advocates, their signature collectors were instructed to avoid any form of confrontation. "When we did find them," comments Jack Kelleher, an IBEW officer in Lowell, "they'd just pick up stakes and leave immediately." While most of the union monitors were able to discourage potential signers at ABC petition sites, it was impossible to cover every location. "We had nine beepers, a hotline, and call forwarding up in the Merrimack Valley," remembers Bill Ryan with frustration. "But they had paid people to be in the industrial parks, elderly housing projects, at dumps. We just couldn't always find them."

Even finding them was not always enough. The

hotline system relied on too few people making too many phone calls and hurried trips to intervene before a significant number of signatures had been gathered. "The ABC instructed people to fold up their tents when we arrived," comments John Malone, a Painters Union officer from the western part of the state. "The hotline slowed them down, but apparently it didn't stop them." The operation depended on too many steps: locating and reporting Fair Wage Committee activity, dispatching union spokespersons, and, finally, discouraging voters who neither knew nor cared much about the still obscure prevailing wage law. "We failed miserably," Carpenters Union official Joe Gangi says bluntly, "because as far as the general public goes we never distinguished the prevailing wage issue from any of the other petitions being circulated at the time." Furthermore, the ABC was better organized and financed than it had been in 1985. "The problem was that they had enough people this time around to persevere," concludes Isakson.

There was another problem that was more fundamental. "We didn't perceive the situation to be as serious as it was," Bill Ryan says. As a result, the hotline remained almost exclusively in the hands of the unions' leadership in too many of the local unions. While many business agents and other officers gave up some evenings and weekends to staff phones and roam shopping malls in their communities, the membership remained largely uninformed about the entire organizational effort. According to

Brian Sanford, business manager of Laborers Local 429, "we probably had only ten percent of the members involved."

The sense of urgency that fired the Question 2 campaign a year later was lacking in the hotline operation. "I barely knew about it," admits Ed Harrison, an electrician who served as a town coordinator in 1988. "It wasn't discussed on the job the way Question 2 was." As president of the North Shore Building Trades Council, Phil Mason sent out twenty-five hundred mailings about the hotline—one of the more active attempts in the state to reach out to union members. Still, he recognizes that more was needed. "We weren't *really* organized. We called people, but we didn't really educate them."

Perfunctory announcements about the hotlines were made at union meetings, but there was no comprehensive commitment to inform and involve the membership. "The information was given out at union meetings, but it was pretty informal," reports ironworker Waldo Banks. "A lot of it didn't stick." The issues involved with the prevailing wage are complex and have been as misunderstood by many inside the building trades as by those outside the industry. Local union leaders who knew in a general way that repeal would hurt their members did not always fully grasp the relationship between the provisions of the law and the overall state of the union sector. They were, as a result, often unable to present the situation clearly enough to motivate the rank and file. The level of concern, therefore, varied from area to area. Also, the ABC had failed before; many were satisfied with the hope that it would fail again. "I wasn't educated on the signature drive," comments operating engineer Jim McCormack. "And to the extent that we thought about it at all on the job, we were betting that they weren't going to get [the number of signatures they needed]."

The years of unrelenting attacks on the prevailing wage law had frustrated a number of union leaders. "It seemed like we were always on the defensive, always chasing them," says Kevin Cotter, business manager of Plumbers Local 12. Joe Nigro, general agent of the Boston Building Trades Council, agrees: "We felt like we had to take the offensive for a change." At a meeting in July 1987, the Boston BTC endorsed the statewide hotline plan, assigned responsibilities to the local unions, and authorized attorney Alec Gray to draft two proposed referendum questions.

"We wanted to counter their initiative," Nigro says. In August the union-sponsored Citizens for Fairness in Public Construction (CFPC) announced its intention to file two initiative petitions of its own. The first would have set a 5-percent cap on the profits of contractors, subcontractors, suppliers, architects, and engineers involved in public construction. The second would have limited the allowable interest rate on credit cards to 2 percent above the prime rate, not to exceed 12 percent.

Both proposals were designed to appeal to consumers and workers and shift the responsibility for the high cost of building away from construction workers. "It is unfair to cut wages," argued the CFPC press release, "when wages have actually become a less significant part of the total cost of construction over the last 30 years. Contractor, planner and consultant profits are the figures inflating the bottom line."[8] The limit on credit-card interest was intended to attract community support and pressure the banks that financed non-union construction projects.

"The idea with these petitions was twofold," according to Nigro. "We were willing to use them as a negotiating tool with the ABC. We'd drop ours if they'd drop theirs. But if they didn't want to, then we wanted to set it up at election time '88 so that the voters could choose between cutting profits or wages." The novel tactic startled the business community. "Nobody can survive on gross profits of 5 percent," exclaimed materials supplier Warren McDonald. Even the Building Trades Employers Association (BTEA), an organization of union contractors that strongly endorsed prevailing wage legislation, was alarmed. Their newsletter reported that the BTEA had "protested this kind of action to the various local building trades unions in the Boston area."[9]

The voters never had an opportunity to choose between profits and wages. The Boston Building Trades Council proposed that the state's twelve hundred union apprentices carry the burden of the campaign. If each apprentice gathered a hundred names, there would be more than enough signatures to qualify for the ballot. But building trades union leaders at the state level opposed the Boston counterpetitions. Evers and others argued that initiating a union signature-collecting program would confuse and hamper the effort to stop the Fair Wage Committee's drive. The Boston BTC decided to proceed with its plan as well as the hotline. The Plumbers Union in Boston, for example, assigned journeymen to the phones and apprentices to the petitions. They turned in four to five thousand names, but the effort was not consistent across the board. In any case, the lack of statewide coordination doomed the petitions to failure. More than thirty thousand names were collected, but the total fell far short of the number required.

Ultimately, the state hotline and the Boston petitions were plagued by the same dilemma—ambitious leadership-designed plans that were not backed up with effective appeals for membership involvement within each trade. "We just didn't do enough education with our members," acknowledges Russ Sheehan. "A lot of them didn't know about the hotline, and they were confused by the different petitions. First we told them not to sign one, then to sign the others. Eventually a lot of them figured they just shouldn't sign anything."

The failure of the unions either to gather enough signatures for their own petitions or to prevent the Fair Wage Committee from successfully completing its signature drive was demoralizing. "We were pretty depressed," admits Joe Dart, president of the Pioneer Valley Building Trades Council. "We felt like we'd done a good job stopping them in the western part of the state, but we still lost the overall battle and were moving into an even more ominous situation." The success of the Fair Wage Committee's tax-saving appeal angered and disturbed union leaders. "Remember," says David Dow of the Boston District Council of Carpenters, "we may have made mistakes, but they lied." Still, the loss was symptomatic of how far the building trades unions needed to travel in order to meet the ABC's challenge. "At a certain point, we knew they were going to get enough signatures, and we weren't," recalls Rich Gambino, a business agent for IBEW 103. "That produced frustration and embarassment. After all, they had no organization, and we supposedly did. Our failure scared us and, I think, ultimately motivated us."

5 | Pulling the Pieces Together

The referendum process in Massachusetts is intricate and time consuming, designed to discourage frivolous ballot measures. Turning over the signatures it had gathered to the secretary of state in December 1987 was not the final step for the ABC. As required by law, the petition was then submitted to the state legislature for further action. On May 3, 1988, the House voted 123 to 24 that repeal of the prevailing wage law "ought not to pass." After years of similar outcomes, the decision came as no surprise. It just placed another small and expected hurdle in the

ABC's path, requiring it to collect 8,421 more signatures by the end of June.

From the union point of view, these developments were largely irrelevant. No one doubted the ABC's ability to produce the additional signatures. Union leaders now faced a much more serious and daunting problem—how to gear up for a full-scale public campaign to defeat a ballot question that would be framed as a tax-saving measure. The implications of the ABC accomplishment sank in slowly. Many building trades officials had continued to hope that the issue would somehow disappear and were now reluctant to face the enormity of the upcoming task. The vast majority of rank-and-file unionists remained completely unaware of ABC activities, the significance of the prevailing wage statute, and the impending threat to their standard of living. "At that time," remarks Tom Williams, president of Laborers Local 133, "most of our members didn't even know what the prevailing wage was." In the fall the hotline had preoccupied active officers and members, but the results of the ABC signature drive produced widespread discouragement. The necessary transition to a political campaign mentality was not an easy or natural step to take. The immediate future promised only an unfamiliar journey into uncharted waters with limited prospects for success.

"In December and January, we started to put together some organization," recalls Joe Dart. "But it was slow. There was no agreement on the financial structure or how the campaign would be designed."

In order to pull the pieces together, Tom Evers invited the officers of all the building trades unions in Massachusetts to a meeting on January 14 in Worcester. Few of those who attended arrived in an optimistic mood. Historically, construction union leaders had far more experience in disagreeing with one another than in working together.

"There were a lot of open questions," points out Phil Mason, "negative feelings left over from the results of the hotline and our counterpetitions, concerns about relations between the Carpenters and the rest of the Building Trades [the Carpenters Union had withdrawn from the Massachusetts Building Trades Council in 1983], and uncertainty over the choice of campaign consultants. A lot of people didn't think it was going to come together."

In Worcester the state Building Trades Council's Executive Board offered a series of recommendations. They proposed that a fifty-dollar assessment be levied on every building trades union member to underwrite the costs of the campaign, that Politics, Inc., a Washington, D.C.–based public relations firm be hired to develop media strategy, and that a campaign committee be established with Arthur Osborn as chair. "At that meeting, the trades formally recognized that we had to broaden the issue and involve the AFL-CIO and the whole House of Labor," comments Dart.

The proposals were followed by discussion from the floor. "I remember that vividly," says Joe Robicheau, a Carpenters Union organizer. "There were a few speakers who rehashed old stuff. Then [former IBEW 103 business manager] Jack Taylor got up and said, 'There's no sense in looking back, we're in a war here, let's just get it together.' He got a standing ovation." According to Joe Sheehan, "That meeting was a turning point. A light went on in everybody's head. That was the first time I started feeling good about what was happening."

The fifty-dollar assessment was initially conceived of as an effective method to raise funds—and it was. The Committee for Quality of Life ultimately raised well over $2 million, a sum that enabled the unions to outspend their opposition by a margin of more than two to one. But, unintentionally, the assessment may have proved to be one of the more farsighted motivational decisions of the campaign. "We obviously needed money," Kevin Cotter notes, "but it could have been raised in a number of ways. The assessment created a psychological investment." Taxing the membership pushed union leaders to explain the issue and justify the expense. For many of the local unions, the meeting to approve the levy was the first occasion on which the implications of a repeal of the prevailing wage law were thoroughly discussed. Bill Foster, a retired bricklayer, stresses the importance of that process. "I suppose the money could have come out of the unions' general funds. In some ways, it's easier to take it out of the kitty. But this way the members became more involved and were more likely to hold our leaders accountable.

Hey, if it comes directly out of our pockets, we're going to pay more attention."

The Worcester meeting had formally requested the assistance and leadership of the state AFL-CIO, and Osborn arrived with an "action plan." "We knew this couldn't be won by the building trades alone," he comments, "or even the labor movement alone. It had to pull in the whole community. Still, the first push had to come from the inside out, from the trades." The plan called for voter registration, education, outreach, and other programs tied together by a "quality of life" theme, a phrase used by state AFL-CIO officers since the early 1980s as part of their political action efforts.

Osborn believed that the campaign needed to be modeled on the state AFL-CIO's previous political work. "Massachusetts has been essentially a one-party state," he says, "and we've felt that we've had to work with Democratic party activists to get labor's message into the communities." At the Democratic party's 1983 state Issues Convention, AFL-CIO delegates successfully steered a fifteen-point Jobs and Justice plank (including support for the prevailing wage law) into the party platform. Two years later their job was a little tougher. The fallout from the Mondale presidential foray had stuck organized labor with the "special interest" tag. National state Democratic officials insisted that the 1985 platform be brief, nonspecific, and free of commitments to the various constituencies within the party.

As a result, labor delegates had to tiptoe more delicately through the political mine fields. The AFL-CIO produced a video that incorporated the sentiments and music of the widely popular song "We Are the World" and challenged the image of labor as a narrow self-interest group by mounting a campaign based on the theme "Our Special Interest Is You." Democratic party leaders, however, remained committed to a bland, generic, and uncontroversial program. The final version of the platform retained planks supporting the prevailing wage law and binding arbitration for public workers—but only as the result of extensive labor pressure.

By the time of the 1987 Issues Convention, Democrats' fear of being labeled as the special-interest party had subsided somewhat. Delegates welcomed a four-point "quality of life" program unveiled by the AFL-CIO that called for universal health care, safe jobs paying good wages, quality education, and affordable housing. John Laughlin of the AFL-CIO says, "We saw the 'quality of life' name as a banner to pull together labor people and folks outside labor on common issues." Once again, backing for the prevailing wage was built into the platform, the centerpiece of the demand for decent jobs.

As the chair of the campaign to preserve the prevailing wage, Osborn suggested that the tactics and themes employed in the issues conventions were transferable to the upcoming referendum battle. "The quality-of-life plank was our way of reaching out to groups outside labor in the Democratic party.

To win an election we were going to have to do the same kind of outreach." Osborn's views prevailed over those who thought that the phrase was bland and vague and shifted the focus away from a clear defense of wages, working people, and unionism. The newly formed campaign organization was named the Committee for Quality of Life.

The first item in the AFL-CIO action plan was a voter registration program. While it is a common component in many electoral campaigns, voter registration was of particular importance in an issue involving construction workers. Participation in electoral activity has been on the decline in recent years, especially among moderate- and lower-income citizens. This trend has profoundly influenced the nation's political direction by granting disproportionate power to voters at the higher end of the income scale. The success of a campaign aimed at protecting a blue-collar wage standard was, therefore, jeopardized by an evolving electorate that skews results away from working-class interests.

Construction workers have been no exception to the rule of declining electoral participation by the working population. If there had been any doubts on this score, the Boston Building Trades Council's profit-cap and credit-card petition drive clearly underlined the reality. Union volunteers who solicited signatures regularly discovered that their coworkers were unable to sign because they were not registered to vote. "What we found was amazing," notes the IBEW's Russ Sheehan. "When our coordinator for the town of Whitman contacted the twenty IBEW members who lived there, for example, he discovered that only five were registered."

Low registration rates may have surprised union officials who had never tried to draw their membership into electoral activity, but it was old news for professional politicians, who survive on data regarding voting patterns and demographic changes. Conventional political assumptions about the inability of labor officialdom to deliver blocs of voters rest, in part, on the perception that "old guard" labor leaders are not in touch with evolving rank-and-file concerns and, in part, on the knowledge that large numbers of union workers do not vote. In a private meeting in the spring of 1988, Representative Joe Kennedy told a group of building trades union officials that he thought the prevailing wage law was in trouble based on figures showing low registration patterns among construction workers.

The Committee for Quality of Life proposed a comprehensive voter registration program with a series of target dates. The plan called for sign-up operations to be established at work sites and public events, as well as an ongoing effort to register unionists and their families. A successful registration operation was the precondition for all other campaign activities. Not only would it create a substantial number of new voters with an obvious commitment to the preservation of the prevailing wage law, but it could double as an educational vehicle to inform the membership of the importance of the upcoming battle. The numbers alone warranted a major investment of resources. Initial polling information generated by the committee revealed that union members and their immediate families added up to 32 percent of the general population.

The committee helped coordinate registration booths at fairs, picnics, and other public gatherings. In addition, volunteers staffed tables at selected factories and offices across the state through arrangements with some of the AFL-CIO's industrial, public, and service sector unions. The bulk of the effort, however, was carried out over a period of months by the individual building trades unions. Some of the larger unions and groups of smaller locals obtained voter lists and kept them at a series of centralized locations. Then the tedious and painstaking work began. Each union's membership list had to be checked, name by name, against the voter books from the 351 towns and cities in Massachusetts.

All the unions developed similar systems. Members' names and registration status were carefully documented, and a record of follow-up phone calls was kept. In Pipefitters Local 537, organizer Dana Kelly recruited apprentices and retirees to help sort the membership of twenty-one hundred according to the 110 towns in which they lived. Full-time officers and volunteer journeymen then operated phone banks during the evening to contact those members whose names did not appear on voter lists. Additional mailings, phone calls, and checks with the various town and city halls confirmed that registration had indeed occurred. Large unions, such as Carpenters Local 33, Plumbers Local 12, IBEW Local 103, and numerous others, set up rank-and-file committees to monitor the registration process. Typically, committee volunteers would be assigned responsibility for the other union members who lived in their community.

Regions with smaller locals pooled their resources and set up programs that crossed trade lines. Hundreds of mailings went out, stewards checked on the job site, anyone who entered a union hall to pay dues was reminded to register, and active officers and members were deputized to serve as registrars. In the Merrimack Valley, Nancy Doherty, a member of Laborers Local 429, registered 125 new voters in one early session. In the Pioneer Valley and the Berkshires, eight well-publicized registration sessions were held on evenings and Saturdays to sign up those individuals who had been identified as not registered to vote. Ultimately, each union tailored its approach to match its particular situation. Laborers Local 22, for example, sent out letters in English, Spanish, and Italian to announce an open-air sidewalk registration day in Boston's North End.

All the unions discovered they had one thing in common. "We decided to do a sample of our members in the town of Hull," says Tom Chirillo of Laborers Local 133. "I was in shock when I saw the numbers." All the predictions of low registration rates proved to be accurate. "Of the hundred pipefitters in my town," Martin Downey of Weymouth points out, "just over a third of us were registered." Bob Munro represents a small union of sixty painters in Lowell. His survey revealed that only four of the local's members were eligible to vote. Not all the unions reported such grim statistics, however. In a few cases, the numbers of registered voters climbed well into the 70-percent range. But overall, fewer than half of all union building trades workers in Massachusetts were registered to vote in early 1988.

Even in the unions with higher levels of registration, the distribution patterns were matters of concern. "In my local," says Bill Ryan of the Operating Engineers, "older members who own their homes in outlying communities were registered in excess of 70 percent. In the towns and cities where we have younger renters who are starting families, it was closer to 50 percent." Similarly, Harvey Isakson of the Sheet Metal Workers noticed that many of his nonregistrants were either apprentices or new members. In general, young workers, in Massachusetts as elsewhere, had failed to keep up with their predecessors. This trend even applied to some union leaders. Ron Rheaume, a thirty-five-year-old organizer for Carpenters Local 1305 in Fall River who played a major role in the campaign, ruefully admits that he did not register until 1988. "For a lot of our younger members, this was their first issue to rally around," theorizes IBEW's Jack Kelleher. "The post-sixties generation had no experience with activism. That's why they weren't registered to vote."

The months of poring over lists, sending letters, making phone calls, and double- and triple-checking voter lists produced a substantial transformation in the rates of voter registration among union members. Laborers Local 473 in Pittsfield boosted its percentage of members who were registered voters from 45 to 90; Carpenters Local 475 in Ashland jumped from under 50 percent to 97 percent; the Boston Pipefitters local moved from 37 percent to 95 percent; and by the campaign's end, every single painter in Munro's Lowell local union was a registered voter. The concentrated outreach extended to union families. "A lot of our members and their spouses were already registered," comments Harry Kalashian of Carpenters Local 111, "but their kids weren't, so we registered them." It would probably be no exaggeration to say that as a result of this program union construction workers in Massachusetts established one of the highest voting registration rates of any demographic group in the state.

The intensity of the program spilled over to other industries as well. Dick Courtney is a business agent with the United Food and Commercial Workers (UFCW) in western Massachusetts. Despite the fact that the workers he represents are not in construction, he played an active and visible role in the prevailing wage campaign. The UFCW conducts periodic registration drives as a matter of course, but, according to Courtney, "our effort in 1988 was more successful than usual since the building trades had gotten all the voter lists and identified who wasn't registered. We were able to benefit from that work."

The voter registration drive was significant for a number of reasons. It heightened awareness of the prevailing wage issue and increased the number of people who would vote no in November. More important, it was the begining of a campaign mode of operation. Union leaders sought out their members, explained the issue, and urged them to register. Rank-and-file volunteers were given an opportunity to be active unionists, no longer outside leadership activities. Unions with a history of occasional antagonism joined forces, sharing voter lists and registration techniques. And, finally, those locals that organized strong volunteer committees had a head start on the development of a field organization for the final months of the campaign. IBEW Local 259 in Salem was just one of a number of local unions that organized their registration programs by town, ward, and precinct because, as Paul L'Heureux put it, "we knew we'd be using that structure later." Rick Brown, who would later serve as the Committee for Quality of Life's coordinator for the town of Gloucester, agreed. "Doing voter registration introduced me to a lot of people in my town that I ended up counting on later, and I started thinking real hard about what lay ahead."

6 | Themes and Tactics

*This referendum is a pretty weapon:
it is nickel-plated with taxpayer
protection and competition
stimulation; but its chambers are
loaded and pointed directly at the
construction trades' unions. . . .
At the heart of this referendum is
plain, old-fashioned union bashing.*
—David Damkoehler,
   Business and Economic Review,
   September 6, 1988

In late April 1988 the Committee for Quality of Life sponsored a series of training sessions for people who were likely to speak on behalf of the campaign. Committee staffers presented materials challenging ABC positions and suggested a variety of approaches that would reinforce the pro–prevailing wage message. This process of internal education was in its infancy, a captive of the slow and painstaking emergence of a campaign organization. "We knew we were right back then," remembers Leo Purcell, who had just been elected to replace the retiring Tom Evers as president of the Massachusetts Building Trades Council. "But we simply didn't have the arguments lined up to support our case. I spoke to a group of senior citizens in Uxbridge in early May. It went fine, but I was struck by how much I still needed to learn about the issue."

The ABC had no such problems. Twenty years of research, organization, and political action across the country had produced a chorus of marketable slogans and political one-liners. Their lobbying efforts in the Massachusetts legislature had refined and honed their message on the local level. The 1987 signature drive initiated their organization into a campaign mode of operation as ABC staffers toured the state promoting the ballot question. A month and a half before the election, Tocco could legitimately say, "We've been out there for a year, talking with the public, talking to Rotary clubs and getting all the endorsements of these various newspapers."[1]

The ABC commissioned a study by the conservative Foundation for Economic Research to develop ammunition for a pro-repeal position. Released in March, the FER report concluded that elimination of the state's prevailing wage law would produce a 14 percent reduction in public construction costs that would translate into $212 million in savings for taxpayers. This assertion was based solely on a "confidential" estimate by one private contractor regarding one small nonresidential structure. In addition, the report arrived at these figures by making the unlikely assumption that contractors would reduce their profits by 10 percent.[2] Despite the fact that the research relied on inappropriate, unrepresentative, and unverifiable data, the FER study was widely cited in media outlets across the state.

The unquestioning acceptance of the FER study revealed the extent of the vacuum that existed in terms of thoughtful discussion of the merits of the prevailing wage statute. A combination of ABC preparation and union disorganization had given repeal advocates a wide-open field. Tocco fed journalists a steady diet of horror stories about projects with outrageous price tags that he attributed to the prevailing wage law. The Committee for Quality of Life was not yet prepared to rebut these charges, thus leaving the gates open for editorialists to take largely unchallenged potshots. When the *Boston Herald* announced its support for the final stage of the ABC's signature drive in May, the newspaper's editorial writer referred to a $300,000 job in Lenox with a $200,000 cost overrun and blithely blamed it on the "legalized larceny" of the prevailing wage law. When Barbara Anderson announced in June that repeal was an indirect way of implementing Proposition $2^{1}/_{2}$, few people were prepared to question if that was desirable, or if, for that matter, the statement was accurate.[3]

One month after the release of the FER report, a *Boston Globe* columnist summed up the common wisdom when he described the prevailing wage law as "a welfare program that taxpayers cannot afford." The ABC achieved a monopoly on the terms of the debate. In June State Senator Michael Barrett (D–Cambridge) insisted to a skeptical reporter that the referendum was not a tax-cut issue. "This is not wiping out the county courthouse gang," he pointed out. "This is not going after outrageous waste. This is a matter of paying people decent wages, and I'm stunned at how misunderstood the issue is."[4]

The Committee for Quality of Life may not have had the information it needed to rebut the ABC's claims early in the campaign, but the weight of the available evidence supported the pro–prevailing wage position. What was needed was a marshaling of resources, strong and credible data, and mechanisms to distribute the information. In March the committee contacted the nationally respected research firm Data Resources, Inc. The agreement that was reached allowed DRI to have complete and final control over methodology and conclusions, regardless of the political implications. The terms of the contract were, in the words of DRI senior economist Doug Poutasse, "an extraordinary thing coming from a client."[5] From the union perspective, it was the only serious option available. A reputable analysis was needed to undermine the FER's patently partisan point of view. DRI's independence would underpin the credibility of its findings. While this stance had its risks, committee leaders were confident that an objective investigation would discredit the tax-savings argument.

Data Resources released its study on August 25. The research firm predicted that the most likely outcome of repeal would be a 0.6 percent tax savings, a $196 million wage loss, an influx of out-of-state contractors and workers, and increased chaos in the construction labor market. Instability is not only a problem in itself, the study pointed out, but it carries a high social cost in terms of increased expenditures on unemployment compensation and workers compensation. "The only clear result of repealing the Massachusetts prevailing wage law," the report's authors concluded, "would be lower wages for Massachusetts residents."[6]

The report confirmed what other observers of the industry had long recognized. If union wage standards were no longer required on state-funded projects, the ripple effect would be staggering. Nonunion wages would quickly serve as the norm on all public construction, because the low bidder would virtually always be the employer with the lowest payroll expenses. Private-sector developers and owners would then object to the double standard and insist that the non-union scale be applied to their projects. The unions would find themselves trapped in a publicly supported bargaining vise; that is, they would be unable to compete on public projects and, eventually, would be frozen out of private-sector development. Lowering the union scale would only benefit employers, as the open-shop rate would continue to be established at a fraction of union pay. Wage concessions in construction across the country have demonstrated a clear pattern: As the union rate plummets, the non-union wage soon follows. For all these and other reasons, the DRI economists insisted that repeal would threaten the standard of living across the board, lower public revenues as taxable income was reduced, and trigger a negative multiplier effect on local economies due to diminished purchasing power.

Perhaps more than any other single development in the campaign, the release of the Data Resources study altered the public debate on the prevailing wage law. Its findings served as the source of many subsequent CQL statements and advertisements, and the firm's integrity cast a long shadow of doubt on the claims of the ABC. The report forced the Fair Wage Committee to backpedal quickly on a year's worth of uncontested allegations. Acknowledging to a reporter that the FER report was "not a scientific study," Tocco moved to deflect the mounting criticism of his position. "I don't think this battle should be over studies," he hedged. "We're talking about a process of buying construction services which is out of whack."[7]

The DRI study was a turning point in the campaign. As the research findings gradually filtered into the media, the terms of the debate began to shift. At the same time, CQL staffers dipped into other wells of information that further repudiated ABC claims. By late summer, the credibility of the Fair Wage Committee was on its way to becoming a major issue of the campaign. The suggested tax savings—the centerpiece of the ABC appeal—looked more and more to be a false hope. The ABC's carefully constructed image as the champion of overburdened taxpayers and fiscally conscious municipal officials was beginning to unravel.

The Fair Wage Committee had succeeded in making hay out of a number of their "horror stories." Perhaps the most controversial anecdote concerned the town of Great Barrington, in western Massachusetts. The Fair Wage Committee's Martin Burke devoted a broadly distributed press release to an account of the bid process for the town's lawn-mowing services. In February 1988 town officials had received a bid of $15,800. A month later the state ruled that new bids had to be solicited in order to comply with the prevailing wage law. When CBN Landscape offered to do the work for $77,100, the ABC realized it had a potential campaign barn-burner. Burke went to work and was able to land a headline in a July edition of the *Berkshire Courier* that read "Lawn Mowing Bids Point up 'Idiocy' of Wage Law."[8]

The supposed Great Barrington boondoggle found its way into nearly every newspaper story on the campaign as well as into ABC television ads. Despite the fact that the higher bid reflected a contractor's high estimate rather than fixed labor costs, the Fair Wage Committee stuck the unions with full responsibility. The irony of the affair was that the bidding process continued until August, and the final result belied the claimed inflationary impact of the prevailing wage law. Great Barrington ultimately signed contracts based on prevailing wages with another firm for $15,100, a $700 savings from the very first bid. But the damage had been done. "There's no question that the lawnmower issue hurt us," comments Pat Mele, Jr., of Laborers Local 473 in Pittsfield. "But the whole thing was based on the contractor and a mistake by the state's Department of Labor and Industries that was corrected." The Committee for Quality of Life publicized the favorable resolution of the case, but the corrected stories in the newspapers never received the same kind of play as the initial accounts.

For months the Fair Wage Committee's operating assumption that *all* construction cost overruns were the result of union pay scales was passively accepted by a docile media. Although labor costs play a limited role in total price projections, few reporters understood the intricacies of construction economics well enough to question ABC allegations. As a result, outlandish arguments were passed off as fact. Tocco could and did suggest that the prevailing wage law added 20 percent to public projects, despite the fact that virtually every reputable study estimates labor to represent a declining share (currently 14 to 20 percent) of total construction costs. Little attention was paid to the mounting materials, overhead, profit, land, and financing costs that play an increasingly pivotal role in the building process.

By the end of the summer, the horror stories no longer went unanswered. When the Fair Wage Committee held a press conference at the Casaubon Senior Center in Southbridge to announce that plans for an addition to the center had been put on hold because the prevailing wage law had pushed up the costs from $140,000 to $400,000, supporters of the law were sufficiently informed and organized to prepare a response. City Councillor Roger Duquett told the press that the figures cited were unrealistic, that the town was trying to get the job done at cut-rate prices, and that there was no guarantee that the work would not have ended up costing more without the law. "We were looking at something for nothing here," he concluded.[9]

The argument over the law's true impact on public projects took on a personal and often vindictive flavor in some of the state's smaller communities. In Uxbridge businessman and selectman Peter Baghdasarian initiated a year-long vendetta against State Representative Richard Moore over the question of the prevailing wage. In widely circulated handwritten fliers, Baghdasarian labeled the statute a "GREED LAW," attacked Moore for his opposition to the referendum, and claimed that a $300,000-plus South Uxbridge fire station could have been built for one-third the cost. "It is clear that the facts do not support such an absurd claim," Moore responded in a letter to the *Blackstone Valley Tribune*. The legislator pointed out that public records showed that materials, equipment rental, professional design services, and other preliminary nonlabor costs alone amounted to nearly $220,000. "Since, as a result of the passage of the Thirteenth Amendment to the U.S. Constitution (abolition of slavery)," Moore continued, "it is necessary to pay people to construct the facility, some additional amount would be needed above the cost of materials."[10] Here, as in most of the other instances cited by the Fair Wage Committee, union wages were not the real issue. At last, opponents of the referendum were making that clear.

The ABC pinned much of its hope on appealing to voters' sympathy for hard-pressed local budgets and to their negative perceptions of building trades workers. Certainly, the standard image of construction workers and their labor organizations was vulnerable to manipulation. Early polling data by the Committee for Quality of Life revealed that 28.6 percent of the sample population held "fairly low" or "very low" opinions of building trades unions. Clearly, a media campaign pitched at negative associations with the stereotypical overpaid, narrow-minded hard hat had the potential to influence public opinion.

In a June newspaper article, Tocco rhetorically asked, "Does the government have the right to guarantee everyone $50,000 a year?"[11] Tocco and other repeal advocates repeatedly raised in every possible forum the specter of the greedy construction worker earning $50,000 a year. The Fair Wage Committee even managed to insert the figure—as if it were fact—into the summary of the pro–Question 2 position in the election handbook issued by the state government. In response, the Committee for Quality of Life released U.S. Department of Labor figures showing that the average Massachusetts construction worker earned $26,734 in 1987. In addition,

CQL officials noted that construction workers' income does not include sick pay or vacation pay and is subject to the vagaries of seasonal employment. As the CQL's statistics began to gain a wider hearing, ABC officials beat a hasty retreat. "Whatever the actual number is," Tocco told an inquiring reporter in October, "our whole point is that the state should not be in the business of guaranteeing wages."[12]

For all the CQL's data, the ultimate discrediting of the Fair Wage Committee's claims came from the final authorities themselves—the "overpaid" construction workers. The $50,000 drumbeat produced a torrent of outraged letters to the editor. Charles Black of Taunton wrote to his local newspaper: "I'm a union ironworker and in my 20 years ironworking I have never made [$50,000] even when combined with my wife's salary." A New Bedford newspaper article described thirty-four-year-old union carpenter Don Raiche, who "drives an 8-year old Oldsmobile and got a mortgage on a house only because the seller was his grandmother. [Raiche] snickers when he hears that he supposedly makes $50,000 a year. 'I don't save any money, let's put it that way.'" The same story quoted Lynn Donohue, president of a firm that employed twenty-five union bricklayers who averaged between $22,000 and $30,000 a year.[13]

The ABC's figures for union wages had indeed infuriated construction workers. Brewster carpenter David Burkitt wrote to the *Cape Codder*: "I have yet to meet one of the '$26 an hour' painters that the pro-repeal ads talk about. . . . Without my wife's income, she and I could not maintain our household. I firmly believe that most critics of the prevailing wage would find it difficult to live on my salary." Individuals outside the industry responded more in amusement than anger. On the eve of the election, Thomas Alecrin of Fall River wrote to the *Sunday Herald News*: "When I heard the average construction wage was $50,000 annually, I was ready to put on my Reeboks and run right down to the Carpenters Union local to begin my apprenticeship training. . . . Several construction workers proceeded to show me pay stubs for several pay periods, which when projected for a full year amounted to $23,000. . . . Needless to say, my vision of becoming a nail banger at a grand a week quickly disappeared."[14]

The DRI report had concluded that lower wages would not necessarily translate into tax savings. In addition, there was no guarantee that repeal would even produce reduced building costs, whether or not those savings were passed on to the taxpayer. In fact, previous experience indicated otherwise. In 1971, in response to spiraling construction costs, President Richard Nixon had suspended the Davis-Bacon Act. Six weeks later the law was reinstated after figures showed that two-thirds of the newly liberated contracts were rebid at the same price or higher. According to John Dunlop, a Nixon administration official and subsequently secretary of labor under President Gerald Ford, "The underlying economy was thrusting these wages forward, and Davis-Bacon had nothing to do with it."[15]

The information generated and disseminated by prevailing wage supporters was painting the Fair Wage Committee's positions in a new and unflattering light. Reporters became increasingly reluctant to take ABC statements at face value. At a September press conference, for example, Tocco was sharply questioned on the tax-savings claim. To the question, "Will every taxpayer get this [money back]?" he replied defensively: "We have never advocated that." Jim Braude, executive director of the Tax Equity Alliance, was even more skeptical. With the 1980 and 1986 ballot measures sponsored by the Citizens for Limited Taxation, he noted, opponents and supporters agreed that the potential tax savings would be significant. They simply differed over the policy value of such cuts. Question 2, he went on, was different. "No such debate need occur. After examining the research of both sides, the inescapable conclusion is that there is no big tax break waiting in the wings."[16]

With the diminishing effectiveness of the tax-savings argument, of the horror stories related to the prevailing wage, of the anecdotes about greedy workers, unionists were able to sharpen the focus on the ABC's underlying motives. If, in fact, the Fair Wage Committee was not going to unburden the weary taxpayer, why were so many resources being applied to the repeal of an obscure piece of legislation? "I find it very interesting," remarked Joe Dart, president of the Pioneer Valley Building Trades Council, "that people who are concerned about tax dollars on construction don't address the issue of profits, real estate charges, bonding issuances and the cost of land. It's the workers they attack." Speaking to another reporter, Dart asked and answered the obvious question. "Why do these people have to go after that [labor] portion? In their quest to save the taxpayers' money, why don't they go after the other 85 percent? I'll tell you why. It's because they represent those other portions of the jobs."[17]

Penetrating the ABC's smoke screen of taxpayer advocacy allowed the unions to paint a more honest picture of the forces behind the Fair Wage Committee. The ABC is, after all, an organization of building employers whose purpose is to operate profitable businesses. In the construction industry, contractors have little or no control over factors like financing, materials, real estate, or insurance costs. Profitability therefore hinges on managerial efficiency, sharp estimating pencils, and limited payroll expenses. While all employers seek to keep a lid on wages, the particular constraints in construction propel the compensation structure into a position of extraordinary prominence.

Non-union builders are perpetually looking over their shoulders at the union sector. Even in areas where the bulk of construction is built open shop, the non-union pay scale is still set in relation to the union standard. Any mechanism that can lower the union rate will lead to reduced wages for unorganized workers and potentially greater profits for non-union contractors. The driving force for repeal of the prevailing wage law was, in the final analysis, the employers' desire to sustain profitability at the expense of a living wage.

At times during the campaign, observers caught a glimpse of the Fair Wage Committee's carefully concealed bottom line. Lawrence Allen, president of the Massachusetts/Rhode Island ABC, revealed some of his organization's motives in a fund-raising appeal. Predicting that upcoming construction projects would require an expanded work force, Allen candidly wrote: "Every one of our member firms will have their workers pirated, stolen and coerced into working for significantly higher wages. If the law is repealed we will be in a better position to compete for the workforce we have to maintain." South Hadley contractor Michael Ciolek offered a variation on the same theme. In an unguarded moment, he told a reporter that non-union builders sometimes shy away from state-financed projects because employees are introduced to higher pay expectations and become reluctant to return to their previous standard. "You spoil 'em," shrugged Ciolek. "It's human nature."[18]

The ABC's allies also understood where the bottom line was located. "The idea is to get the lowest rate possible. If this affects wages," commented Barbara Anderson, it is not the "worry" of local government. When a Medford alderman justified support for Question 2 by explaining that "if a developer of a construction site can have two workers for the price of one, then that's two people who have work instead of one," Massachusetts Secretary of Labor Paul Eustace blew up in exasperation. In a letter to the Medford newspaper, Eustace exclaimed: "The implications of that remark are staggering. Most people in this economy can barely make ends meet now. Should public policy be geared to reducing wages in the name of generating more jobs?"[19]

The Committee for Quality of Life managed to accomplish a difficult political task. Union advocates turned the tables on the ABC, transforming what had been widely accepted as a tax issue into a referendum on wages, profits, and the rights of working people. In an era when tax- and budget-cutters reign supreme, accepting the Fair Wage Committee's definition of the repeal issue would have been an act of political suicide for the unions. By the end of the campaign, large numbers of voters had been disabused of the notion that repeal of the prevailing wage law equaled lower tax bills. Instead, many members of the public agreed with tax expert Jim Braude when he announced that, if the prevailing wage law were repealed, "[our] conclusion is that the pocketbooks of thousands of working families will shrink while the only pocketbooks which may grow fatter are contractors'."[20]

7 | Building Bridges

The ABC conceived of, directed, and underwrote the Fair Wage Committee. ABC member firms provided the bulk of the financing for the committee's campaign activities, with nearly one-quarter of the total revenues coming from non-union contractors located outside Massachusetts. Question 2 was strictly an employer-funded referendum. "Of the 109 original Fair Wage contributors, only 9 were people," notes the AFL-CIO's John Laughlin. "The other hundred names either ended in Inc., Co., or Ltd."

Although ABC members carried the financial

load, other political and business organizations had a strong interest in the success of the referendum. The presidential campaign offered Republican leaders an opportunity to tie the local ballot question to the national opposition to Davis-Bacon. Andrew Card, a former mechanical contractor, served as George Bush's campaign manager for the Northeast. A long-time opponent of the prevailing wage law who was later appointed deputy White House chief of staff, Card told *Engineering News-Record* in August that Bush's staff actively supported Question 2.[1]

Traditional business allies of the ABC in Massachusetts—the High Technology Council and the Chambers of Commerce—maintained their staunch anti-unionism and spoke repeatedly in favor of the ballot measure. Leading political officials, by and large, stood on the union side of the fence. With the exception of the Massachusetts Municipal Association, the majority of elected officials in Massachusetts eventually urged voters to reject repeal. The MMA, an organization of the state's mayors, selectmen, managers, and city councillors, was the only bipartisan political group actively to call for the elimination of the prevailing wage.

The MMA's endorsement was an important political prize. The organization's stance enabled the Fair Wage Committee to claim to represent the interests of fiscally strapped cities and towns. As the campaign wore on and the Fair Wage Committee sought to de-emphasize its ties to the business community, the MMA was increasingly moved to the fore. Not all MMA members were pleased with this development. "The endorsement was made at a Board of Directors meeting instead of at the annual policy meetings where major decisions are supposed to be made," remembers John Walsh, a selectman from Abington. "In the board, decisions can be driven by the Selectmen's Association, a small group of conservative and unrepresentative selectmen from wealthy towns. . . . The endorsement was a little aggravating, but when we took a leading role with TV ads and all the rest, that was outrageous. No polling of the members was ever done, and most of the selectmen and mayors I know ended up supporting the no position on their own." Ultimately, more than two-thirds of the state's mayors ignored the MMA endorsement and took positions opposing Question 2.

In the final analysis, corporate funding and a few key organizational endorsements do not decide elections. Voters do. ABC strategists primarily counted on the tax-savings appeal to sway public opinion, but they also recognized that targeting specific voter blocs would aid their cause. Dating back to the initial legislative campaigns at the State House, ABC officials had attempted to woo public-sector employees and their unions. They hoped to capitalize on two political dynamics. First, public workers still resented the electoral support many construction workers had provided Proposition $2^1/_2$ in 1980. Second, the ABC never failed to remind state and municipal workers that the public pie was limited and that their share might be reduced due to the high cost of public construction projects.

In an August interview, Tocco fanned the flames: "We have teachers earning $18,000 a year, and we pay a painter $50,000? I think that borders on being immoral."[2] The irony of Tocco's statement was that it was not only factually incorrect—the teacher's pay cited is a starting salary that would appropriately compare to a starting apprentice carpenter's income in Springfield of $12,440—but the greatest single cause of low public wage standards has been the successful work of Tocco's steadfast ally, the Citizens for Limited Taxation.

The appeal to public workers emerged as a routine campaign theme. As Richard Boutiette, president of the Massachusetts Highway Association and a leading Question 2 supporter, insisted: "Many of the municipal workers or teachers threatened with layoffs because of Proposition 2½ wouldn't be if the town wasn't forced to waste money on artificially inflated wages." Kevin Costello of the South Shore Chamber of Commerce made the link even more explicit: "The prevailing wage law gives cities and towns a choice: Stop all infrastructure repair and local renovation projects; or, lay off more teachers, cut snow plowing, and hold the line on mediocre salaries for police in order to accommodate the ridiculously inflated wages for public construction."[3]

The ABC's attempts to pit public employees against building trades workers did not pan out, but some fence-mending on the union side had to take place before public workers could be persuaded to join the opposition to Question 2. In one of his first official campaign actions, Arthur Osborn met with the president of the Massachusetts Teachers Association (MTA) and subsequently addressed the group's annual convention. Such overtures to public sector workers proved critical, particularly in the case of the MTA, which is not affiliated with the AFL-CIO. Still, due to old scars, many public employees were initially unwilling to support the building trades workers, and the Committee for Quality of Life had to overcome this reluctance. According to Jonathan Tuttle, a staff representative for the American Federation of State, County and Municipal Employees (AFSCME) Council 93 who played an active role in the campaign in western Massachusetts, "A lot of our people—leaders and members—were asking, 'Where were the building trades when we needed them?'"

Many building trades union officials frankly acknowledged their lack of leadership eight years earlier. "We thought of $2^{1}/_{2}$ as a failure on our part," admits John Malone, business agent for Painters Local 257. "We had to make up for it." In any case, the reality of common interests in the present outweighed the divisive past. AFSCME's Executive Director Joseph Bonavita delivered an endorsement of the prevailing wage law in the March/April issue of the union's newspaper. The National Association of Government Employees followed suit in the summer. Paul Devlin, director of the Massachusetts Federation of Teachers (MFT), directly attacked those who suggested that money for education had to come out of the pockets of construction workers. "I abhor the cynicism that would have us believe that to continue one group's goals, you must cannibalize another's." Stephen Wollmer of the Massachusetts Teachers Association pointed out that while teachers may not earn enough, they don't begrudge building trades workers their wages. "That would be like the person with a bad arm who prays, 'God, make my arm like the other one,' and then the other one goes limp."[4]

The large Service Employees International Union Local 285, two-thirds of whose members are in the public sector, pitched in with leaflets, phone calls, mailings, and a gamut of campaign-related activities. "When our members were appealed to as working people, they understood it was in their interest," suggests SEIU 285 Director Nancy Mills. "They got excited because there was a basic us versus them mentality." Numerous public workers unions went beyond distributing Committee for Quality of Life material and developed their own initiatives. A firefighters union in Cambridge, for example, took out an ad in the local newspaper with a silhouette of a firefighter beside a "Vote No on 2" message.

Direct contact between individual building trades workers and public employees proved particularly effective. Building trades activists addressed countless meetings across the state. In New Bedford and Fall River, campaign volunteers stuffed anti-repeal literature in every public school teacher's mailbox. "The Citizens for Limited Taxation became the common bond between us and public sector workers," claims Paul L'Heureux, a Salem electrician who spoke to teachers, firefighters, police, postal workers, senior citizen groups, and the Democratic Committee in his city. "You just mentioned Barbara Anderson's name and their heads snapped up. They had suffered the most from $2\frac{1}{2}$. They recognized this as an attack on all organized labor and [a no vote on Question 2] as a way of getting even with Anderson."

Industrial unions responded as well. The Committee for Quality of Life supplied each AFL-CIO affiliate with voter registration packets, a full complement of campaign materials, and information for internal newsletters and bulletin boards. Individual building trades unionists augmented the committee's top-down activities with grass-roots contacts through visits to workplaces and local union meetings. The built-in mobility of the construction industry employee came in handy for these connections, particularly in cases where projects were additions to or renovations of functioning work sites. During much of the campaign, for example, pipefitter Martin Downey worked at a construction site connected to the giant Raytheon plant. Before and after work, he distributed literature and spoke to the IBEW 1505 members employed there.

"It wasn't just union people we talked to," says Paul Deane, a Quincy bricklayer. "We spent time talking to non-union people, especially in construction. They knew they were getting $13 or $15 or $16 because of our rates. Plus a lot of them have gotten the union scale on prevailing rate jobs and they know why. How could they vote yes?" Deane was right. As a non-union electrician told a *Boston Phoenix* reporter, the prevailing wage underpinned his way of life. "I'd never be able to afford my mortgage if it goes," he said.[5] On a Saturday late in the campaign, Tom Williams and a number of volunteers leafletted five non-union building sites on the South Shore with a committee-produced flier aimed at unorganized construction workers. "All of the employers were contributors to the Fair Wage Committee," Williams comments, "but the workers were all with us."

Lining up solid union support was imperative, but union support alone was not nearly enough to pull off an electoral victory. A win in November hinged on the creation of a coalition that could transform the prevailing wage battle from a union issue into a community and class issue. On the most obvious level, a coalition was a precondition for success given the low and declining numbers of unionized workers in the work force. In order to achieve the magic goal of 50 percent plus one, hundreds of thousands of voters outside organized labor would have to choose to pull the "no" lever on Question 2. Beyond the simple numbers game, however, the only way to overcome the tax-savings argument was to capture the imagination of the public by asking people to identify with those who would be hurt by re-

peal. Making that empathetic leap required inter-
mediaries—both individual leaders and established
organizations who were prepared to say publicly
that their interests and the larger public interest
would not be served by the success of Question 2.

As it had for the previous five years, the state
AFL-CIO looked to the Democratic party for representation on a range of political issues. On January
29 Osborn and several other union leaders attended
a statewide meeting of the Democratic State Committee. Their appearance produced a unanimous re-
affirmation of the party's support for the prevailing
wage law. In March the Committee for Quality of
Life sent letters signed by a group of labor and political leaders to every delegate to the upcoming Democratic state convention. For reasons concerned both
with timing and with politics, the committee had
targeted the June 11 convention as the official campaign kickoff. With few hotly contested candidate
elections in Massachusetts, the presidential aspirations of Governor Michael Dukakis and the battle
over Question 2 took center stage at the Boston Garden.

The committee organized labor delegates to represent each of the state's forty senatorial districts
and assigned them to distribute and collect pledge
cards from the full gathering of party activists. In
addition to the floor operation, the committee sus-
tained a high profile throughout the convention, un-
veiling the campaign's video presentation and cul-
minating with a display of unity in which Osborn

and AFL-CIO Secretary–Treasurer Robert Haynes were joined at the podium by Lieutenant Governor Evelyn Murphy, State Representative Raymond Jordan of the Black Legislative Caucus, MTA President Nancy Finkelstein, Elsie Frank of the Massachusetts Association of Older Americans, MFT head Paul Devlin, and Alex Rodriguez of the Massachusetts Commission Against Discrimination.

Nearly unanimous support of the Democratic political establishment gave the campaign a helpful jump start. Governor Dukakis and Senators Edward Kennedy and John Kerry delivered clear endorsements. The solid backing of major state officials, as well as urban mayors like Boston's Ray Flynn, Fall River's Carlton Viveiros, and Springfield's Richard Neal, lent credibility and resources to the opposition to Question 2. As momentum built in the fall and a union victory seemed possible, politicians across the state sought to identify themselves with the campaign. Many ward committees, school committees, and city councils passed resolutions opposing Question 2. In Cambridge State Senator Michael Barrett and State Representative Charles Flaherty served as honorary chairs of the town's Quality of Life Committee; at the other end of the state, the Pittsfield City Council unanimously called for defeat of the referendum as Councillor Peter Arlos stated: "Ten percent of the people in this country control eighty-six percent of the assets. We ought to be concerned about people who are working for a living."[6] Six South Shore political leaders appeared in a full-page

98

ad in the *Brockton Enterprise* urging a "no" vote; and elected officials donated office space, appeared at rallies, and spoke at town meetings on behalf of the committee. These associations were mutually beneficial. By the end of the campaign, public figures were eager to appeal to their working-class constituencies on an issue that could be a winner, and the endorsements—particularly from local officials—helped the campaign undercut the impact of the MMA's support for the Fair Wage Committee.

Just as significant, the Committee for Quality of Life opted for a strategy that departed from strictly traditional political endorsements and sought the support of a broad range of grass-roots organizations. One of the earliest such endorsements came from the eighty-thousand-member Citizen Action, the state's largest consumer advocacy organization. "Their early support was important," says John Laughlin. "When the ABC would say this was not a consumer issue, we would say, 'What do you mean? We've got the endorsement of the largest consumer group in the state!'" Citizen Action sent out a mailing to its full membership labeling the ABC as "a tiny special interest group" and trained a number of its most active members to serve as spokespersons for the campaign.

Elsie Frank, Manny Weiner, and other recognized leaders in the state's senior community joined the campaign in its formative stages. Their stance in support of the prevailing wage law carried considerable weight in a variety of critical forums. When the

Shrewsbury *Voice* adopted a pro-repeal editorial position, Shrewsbury resident and coordinator of the AFL-CIO retiree program Ken Mangan visited the newspaper's offices. Armed with the Data Resources report and committee fact sheets, Mangan persuaded the editors to publish the anti-repeal arguments and withdraw their previous endorsement.[7] Joe Walsh of Plumbers Local 12 spoke to United Auto Workers retirees in Framingham, distributed literature during bingo games at senior centers, and arranged dozens of informational presentations at elderly housing complexes. In the final stages of the campaign, the committee mailed fifty thousand brochures with a "Vote No" message from Congressman Claude Pepper to senior citizens across the state.

At the other end of the age spectrum, students on state and community college campuses and in the college towns of Amherst, Northampton, Cambridge, and sections of Boston participated in the campaign. At Harvard students had already received an in-depth education in unionism as a result of the painstaking and ultimately successful organizing drive of the university's employees. The remarkable efforts of the Harvard University Clerical and Technical Workers (HUCTW) organization had generated substantial student sympathy for the union cause. HUCTW organizers welcomed Quality of Life volunteers at all their rallies and helped coordinate student activity in opposition to Question 2.

A student columnist in the *Harvard Crimson* described the referendum as "not only anti-labor, but anti-community. . . . The prevailing wage law is as important to the labor movement as child labor laws, Right-to-Know laws, and the minimum wage. To vote for the repeal is to express a belief that the government should not provide a safeguard for large numbers of productive citizens—in this case labor—against the selfish interests of the few—the contractors."[8] "HUCTW taught unionism to students," claims Cambridge coordinator Steve Krasner. "The work they did over the years had a significant impact on our campaign." Krasner's assertion is supported by the election results. In the Cambridge precinct covering the Harvard dormitories, the referendum was turned down 3½ to 1.

Four days before the election, the Catholic church weighed in. The Right Reverend Monsignor William Murphy expressed his opposition to the ballot question in a column in *The Pilot*. The Labor Guild of the Archdiocese of Boston had taken a similar position considerably earlier, but Murphy's statement carried with it the full authority of the archdiocese and its leader, Cardinal Bernard Law. Despite the lateness of the hour, copies of the article were mailed to every area parish in the hope that priests would incorporate the message into their last sermons before the election. Organizations representing other religious traditions also took a stand. The Jewish Labor Committee, for example, established a sizable committee of supporters inside and outside the labor movement. The committee sponsored educational programs on the referendum and bought a half-page ad in the November 3 issue of the *Jewish Advocate*.

Endorsing organizations ran the gamut: the Massachusetts Nurses Association, the Coalition of Police, Mass Freeze, the Democratic Socialists of America, and the list goes on. Support came from some unexpected quarters as well. Reagan appointee John Thomas Flynn, New England regional chief of the U.S. Department of Labor, issued a strong denunciation of the repeal effort that demonstrated a surprising sensitivity to the reality of working life in the construction industry. In a statement widely reported in the press, Flynn challenged ABC cost-savings claims and suggested that the genuine issues of quality and safety were being lost in the shuffle. Why cut publicly established workers' wages, he asked rhetorically, rather than taxpayer-subsidized "corporate country club privileges, company cars, sky boxes and season tickets with box seats, not to mention business lunches, dinner and other 'entertainment' expenses?" Flynn concluded by mocking the ABC's attitude toward building trades workers, which he described this way: "But what the hell, they just work with their hands. Why should they make that kind of money?"[9]

Several construction employer organizations refused to line up with the ABC. The Massachusetts Council of Construction Employers and the Massachusetts Construction Advancement Program endorsed the Committee for Quality of Life. Peter Volpe, president of Volpe Construction Company, a union firm, wrote op-ed pieces and made public appearances in opposition to the referendum. "Prevailing wage," he wrote, "from a business prospectus, is a sound investment that secures a company's future." In an article in the *Boston Globe*, Tom Gunning, executive director of the Boston Building Trades Employers Association, called on municipal officials to "resist the temptation to buy public works on the cheap." With Question 2, he continued, "we are looking at one portion of one industry seeking to make a higher profit at the expense of every other business, worker and taxpayer in the community."[10]

Not all the CQL's endorsements came easily or automatically. Many leaders of housing and tenant organizations, for example, found themselves torn between their basic sympathies with labor and their concern over the high cost of housing construction. Early in the campaign, for example, Earl Wilcox, a housing rehabilitation specialist for Nueva Esperanza in South Holyoke, told a reporter that, despite his personal support for trade unions, he thought repeal of the prevailing wage law might help his organization. In a letter to Arthur Osborn, the Massachusetts Tenants Organization (MTO) similarly urged that the "wage issue must be evaluated where nonprofit developers are stretching every cent to make a project fly." As Matthew Thall, executive director of the Fenway Community Development

Corporation, explained, "Clearly any group whose principal purpose is to create affordable housing is looking for any way it can to reduce production costs. Even groups that are strongly pro-union and pro-labor because of their membership realize there is a dilemma here."[11]

Thall and the MTO, however, came to a different conclusion from Wilcox's. Concerns about the housing affordability crisis in Massachusetts notwithstanding, the Fenway CDC opposed repeal because, in Thall's words, "People feel this is an assault on unions, and they don't want to support that."[12] Similarly, the MTO, while urging unions to play a bigger role in the production of affordable housing, unconditionally endorsed the Committee for Quality of Life and provided volunteers in the late stages of the campaign.

In response to housing activists' concerns, repeal opponents suggested that the impact of the prevailing wage statute on housing costs was being exaggerated. As Paul Eustace wrote: "In the private housing construction market, for example, non-union contractors paying substandard wages dominate the market. Does anyone think that has done away with the inflated cost of housing in Massachusetts?" Furthermore, the only players in the construction industry to make a significant contribution to the development of affordable housing can be found in the union sector. The Bricklayers and Laborers Non-Profit Housing Company has erected a series of nationally recognized, well-designed, affordable projects in the

Boston area. The First Trade Union Savings Bank, created by the Carpenters Union, has financed a number of affordable housing developments. And union-based nonprofit housing development corporations have been established in Salem, Springfield, and Charlestown.

By the later stages of the campaign, few housing advocates continued to argue that repeal would benefit their organizations. "For people to afford housing these days, wages have to go up," noted Lew Finfer of the Massachusetts Affordable Housing Alliance. "Repeal could lower wages. And we're skeptical of claims that it will save the taxpayers money." The issue of reduced wages and purchasing power was critical. After all, in many cases the very workers whose wages were under attack were the potential buyers of new units of affordable housing. Or as Tom Cunha, president of the Charlestown Economic Development Corporation, succinctly put it: "How do you build affordable housing if the people you're building it for can't afford to buy it?"[13]

Enlisting the support of organizations representing minorities and women proved to be the most complicated piece of the coalition puzzle. In this case the barriers were not a matter of economic arguments but of deeply felt historical and political concerns regarding exclusionary industry practices. Construction is and has been a largely white male world. The difficulty in winning access to construction jobs has convinced many women and minority activists that whatever change has occurred has come only as the result of court action or externally imposed public policies. The result is a legacy of distance and hostility between those activists and industry leaders, including union officials.

Racial and sexual discrimination is a bitter reality in nearly every occupation and industry, but construction has long been a particular target of affirmative action advocates. According to Bill Fletcher, organizer for District 65/United Auto Workers and chairperson of the Community Task Force on Construction, one of the reasons for this is the high visibility of the work. "When people see suburban and out-of-state workers out there on a site in the minority community, the lack of black faces is much more obvious than it is inside an office building out of public view." In addition, construction has served as a traditional path for advancement for successive waves of immigrant groups without higher educational skills. "There's an obvious appeal to blacks," continues Fletcher. "The building trades represent one of the few mechanisms in which workers can earn a decent living and potentially have the freedom to start their own business after learning the trade. Most industries open to minority workers are locked into dead-end paths."

While most job initiatives target employer practices, the focus in construction includes labor organizations because of the unions' input into decisions to admit new members and apprentices. One approach to admission policies—the notion that limits on union membership will protect workers by easing the chronic problem of cyclical unemployment in construction—has led to, in the words of IBEW Organizing Director Mike Lucas, "country-club unionism," an orientation that has, at times, excluded both non-union construction workers as well as potential new entrants to the trades.[14] "Before 1970," comments Joe Nigro, general agent of the Boston Building Trades Council, "there's no question that the doors were closed to our unions. It was pretty much of a father–son arrangement." Fletcher points to the irony of one craft union that maintained its office in the heart of Boston's African-American community without a single black member until 1968. Nigro and other union leaders argue, however, that the once-exclusive building trades unions have opened their doors. Statistics demonstrate that progress has been made in Massachusetts since that era, but disagreement persists about what constitutes an adequate pace of change and whether unions have willingly initiated or reluctantly accepted new programs.

Minorities and women are underrepresented in the construction industry. The most recent figures (from 1985 to 1987) indicate that while African-Americans, Hispanics, and Asians accounted for 6.0 percent of the work force in all industries in Massachusetts, they made up 4.8 percent of the construction work force. In the city of Boston, the minority share of total employment was 24.1 percent, as compared to 23.3 percent in construction. Women have a far weaker foothold in the industry. In 1987 women

107

made up 44 percent of the national work force but held only 8.3 percent of construction jobs and just 1.3 percent of all construction craft–related jobs. Data from Massachusetts reveal that women have doubled their representation in the building trades from 1980 to 1986, but this shift is attributable more to the low 1980 figures than to a rapid influx of new female workers.[15]

The hotly contested question of access occupies a significant place in current employment policy discussions. The Commonwealth of Massachusetts is embarking on a series of massive public works projects—the depression of the Central Artery, construction of the Third Harbor Tunnel, and the cleanup of Boston Harbor—that could potentially add $10 billion worth of new construction to the area's economy. Community activists as well as some state and city policymakers have indicated that they would like to see the jobs generated by these projects filled by a work force that more closely mirrors the general population.

In the most thorough study of the current situation in construction hiring, the Social Policy Research Group (SPRG) investigated the twenty-two-month-long Southwest Corridor Project, the largest and costliest public works project in Boston's history. State officials had set employment goals of 30 percent for minorities and 6.9 percent for women on the union-built Corridor. According to the SPRG, contractors on the project exceeded the minority-hiring target by 5 percent but did not achieve the goal for women. The report also revealed a number of other important industry trends as it branched out beyond the confines of the Corridor Project to survey the general state of affirmative action in Boston construction.[16]

In their recommendations, the authors called for strengthened affirmative action efforts but concluded that long-term careers in construction had become more available to groups historically excluded from the industry. There is, the report stated, "clear evidence that once minorities and women have *entered* the industry, they have been just as likely as white males to stay in it." Furthermore, job stability proved far more typical of the union than the non-union sector. Of the union members surveyed, 97 percent were still in the local construction industry three years later, as contrasted to 65 percent of non-union workers.[17]

"In terms of the goals of affirmative action, we need to look at the new trainees in apprenticeship programs," insists Joe Nigro. "That will determine who has the future careers in construction." In 1988 minorities made up 10.8 percent, and women 4.9 percent, of the apprentices in statewide union-based programs. In programs involving Boston-based local unions (most of whose geographical jurisdictions extend beyond the city and well into other sections of Massachusetts), the percentage of minority apprentices was 13.3, that of women apprentices, 4.9. Individual trades, such as the bricklayers, carpenters, and a number of other unions, have instituted successful pre-apprentice programs, targeted at urban communities, to introduce basic construction-related skills and feed graduates into the standard apprenticeship stream. Similarly, the Boston building trades unions have ties to and draw new apprentices from the Women in the Building Trades program.

Statewide, union minority apprentice figures now exceed the proportion of minorities in the work force overall. The debate continues, but information from the SPRG study, apprenticeship and pre-apprenticeship statistics, and other relevant research demonstrate that while the entire industry may resist change, the union sector has a better record on affirmative action than the non-union sector has. Registration figures for 1988 from ABC-sponsored training programs, for example, show participation rates of 3.0 percent for minority and 2.2 percent for women apprentices.[18]

Inevitably, these long-standing tensions served as a backdrop to the coalition-building strategies of the Committee for Quality of Life. "We knew we might have some problems with groups representing women and minorities," admits Arthur Osborn. On a pragmatic level, the sheer numbers of the constituencies involved made their endorsements a crucial piece of the coalition effort. But beyond the question of numbers, the committee's message of community versus corporate interests could have credibility only if all sectors of the working community were represented. A campaign that staked out its political turf on the side of social and economic justice had no legitimacy without the support of women's and minority organizations.

Other labor unions with a membership primarily made up of women and minority workers expressed concern that the campaign represent the perspectives of the entire organized work force and not just building trades workers. While repeal of the prevailing wage law would initially affect only construction workers, others in the ranks of organized labor recognized that the long-term consequences of repeal would ultimately drive down all wages and potentially create a favorable political climate for right-to-work legislation. Accordingly, eight representatives of private and public sector local unions met with Osborn in early April to insist that both the internal structure and the public face of the campaign reflect the racial and sexual diversity of the local work force.

In response, the committee hired consultant Robin Leeds to work full time on outreach to the minority and women's communities. Janet Walker, president of the American Federation of Government Employees Local 1164, was appointed to the Campaign Steering Committee, and Bill Fletcher was invited to join the Campaign Action Committee. In a series of memos, Leeds proposed a program of coalition building that would identify the prevailing wage law as an issue with clear positive benefits for the constituencies represented by women's and minority organizations.

The committee sought the support of elected officials and grass-roots organizations. Lieutenant Governor Evelyn Murphy provided one of the committee's earliest public endorsements. In July Representatives Suzanne Bump and Frances Alexander and State Senator Lois Pines organized a seminar on the prevailing wage for women legislators. By the fall enough groundwork had been done to win endorsements from the National Organization for Women (NOW), the Massachusetts Women's Political Caucus, the Coalition for Pay Equity, Women for Economic Justice, the Coalition of Labor Union Women, and a number of other organizations. In her statement of support, NOW President Molly Yard argued: "It is ironic that as the construction trades are opening up to women seeking jobs, the owners should try to repeal the longstanding prevailing wage structure which provides a decent wage. Women want these wages for themselves and for all the men working in these trades. We will not be a party to divide and conquer tactics but will stand with the coalitions which comprise the Quality of Life Committee."[19]

Virtually all the statements of support from women's organizations recognized the relevance of prevailing wage legislation to the principle of equal pay for equal work. By requiring contractors to pay *all* employees in each trade predetermined and identical wages, the prevailing wage law is, as SEIU 285 President Celia Wcislo wrote, "the only law on the books that guarantees pay equity for the job . . . regardless of sex, race or union membership." In a flier entitled "How Can We Raise the Floor When the Roof Is Caving In?" Wcislo argued that the prevailing wage law could serve as a model for women organizing in other settings. "The fact that construction firms are mandated by law to set a standard rate of pay is progressive," Wcislo claimed, "and something many of us would love to see in our own occupation or industry. It is a goal that should be broadened; not something that should be taken away from the few who are lucky to have the protection."[20]

Pressure on campaign leaders to incorporate women's concerns came primarily from political and labor spokeswomen outside the trades. While women who work in construction were not drawn sufficiently into the policymaking process, they played a critical role in the campaign—as participants in television and radio ads, as public speakers, and as activists in the field organization. Because their entry into the trades had been more difficult than male workers', their awareness of the referendum's potential damage was keener. "Repealing the Prevailing Wage Law," commented Bernadette Higgins, an apprentice painter who served as campaign coordinator for the town of Medford, "would be literally setting women and people of color back where they started."[21] The endorsements of a wide range of women's organizations extended the campaign's electoral coalition, but the visible presence of tradeswomen in their communities changed the face of the campaign in the streets. "A lot of us hadn't had that much contact with some of the women's organizations," comments Maggie Kirby, a bricklayer and ward coordinator in Boston. "But we pulled a lot of stuff together out of proportion to our numbers. Every tradeswoman I know was involved in the campaign."

The committee undertook a parallel approach with groups representing people of color. Despite some initial endorsements from individual political leaders, the process of cementing links with minority organizations was slow and arduous. In the spring of 1988, representatives of the Community Task Force on Construction (CTFC) met with Joe Nigro, national AFL-CIO staffer Ron Martin (who was working with the Committee for Quality of Life on voter registration), and several other Boston building trades leaders. The group sought to draft a joint statement that would declare support for the prevailing wage law along with a union commitment to increased access and strengthened enforcement of the Boston Resident Jobs Ordinance (which requires that 50 percent of the work force on city-funded construction projects be residents, 25 percent minorities, and 10 percent women).

By early summer, the CTFC had decided to merge its efforts with the parallel activities of the Massachusetts Black Legislative Caucus (MBLC). On June 23 the caucus and the William Monroe Trotter Institute cosponsored a one-day conference on the prevailing wage issue at the University of Massachusetts in Boston. The well-attended session included black elected officials, community leaders, and a group of black union construction workers who took the day off to speak in opposition to the referendum. In one of the two panel discussions of the day, Arthur Osborn and Stephen Tocco debated the ballot question. The decision to invite both men "symbolized where we were at that time," notes Robin Leeds. "The caucus wanted to hear both sides." By the end of the day, the group consensus was leaning in the direction of support for the union position provided that labor made a commitment to work for increased jobs and training programs for minorities.

The Trotter Institute conference raised an issue that would cloud the campaign for a number of months. In his speech Osborn favorably contrasted the unions' record on affirmative action with the ABC's inaction. Reflecting past grievances, many of the conference participants subsequently requested additional information on the numbers of minority workers in each of the various building trades unions. This request had been echoed by representatives of many of the women's organizations involved with the campaign. On July 20 Osborn sent out a letter asking local building trades unions to provide the appropriate information and assigned Nigro the responsibility of collecting the material.

Nigro's task was complicated by the fact that some of the unions in his jurisdiction were reluctant to divulge the statistics. Their decision stemmed, in part, from an unwillingness to make membership lists public for any purpose and, in part, from a fear that a poor showing on minority participation would be used to embarrass individual locals. As a result, Nigro was able to turn over a complete breakdown of apprentices trade by trade but complete figures of the full membership for only twenty-two out of the thirty-one local unions affiliated with the Boston Building Trades Council. Those numbers revealed that, of the twenty-one thousand union members, three thousand were minorities and five hundred were women.

Nigro's inability to produce all the numbers as requested stalemated negotiations between the Committee for Quality of Life and the Black Legislative Caucus for much of the summer. While there was never any intention of supporting the referendum, some minority leaders advocated a neutral position in the absence of a forthright response. The logjam was not broken until late September. In a letter to Osborn, MBLC spokesman and state representative Augusto Grace proposed a new format for an agreement. Grace affirmed the areas of joint work that already existed and outlined a series of future goals for issues that remained unresolved. Subsequent meetings, proposals and counterproposals finally produced what Grace termed a "historic agreement." Announcing the support of the caucus for the prevailing wage law, Grace wrote: "We have made a commitment to a working partnership now and for the future. The Black Legislative Caucus realizes the devastating impact the repeal of prevailing wage would have on working people across the Common-wealth. We are pleased to inform you that we have endorsed the Committee for Quality of Life VOTE NO ON 2 campaign."[22]

The agreement highlighted a number of joint efforts—some already in place, others to be carried out. Commitments were made to bolster vocational training programs in the Boston public schools' Humphrey Occupational Resource Center; to endorse and participate in the Building Opportunities Program, a state project to increase the numbers of minority and female apprentices; to ensure effective monitoring of the Boston Residents Job Ordinance; and to create forums for future joint discussions. The agreement did not produce universal satisfaction, however. Some caucus members as well as other community activists viewed the final step of the process as an unnecessary tactical retreat and as a missed opportunity for firmer commitments at one of the few times when the building trades unions were actively seeking minority support.[23]

As part of the endorsement, the caucus arranged for the Reverend Jesse Jackson to tape a commercial that aired on black radio stations in the final two weeks of the campaign. Jackson's message—"The battleground for workers' rights is the battleground for civil rights. When you cut wages you kill hope! Keep hope alive. Vote No on 2"—was incorporated into a brochure that was mailed to community activists and distributed door-to-door in black neighborhoods. The lengthy and difficult negotiations with the caucus challenged and ultimately transformed the campaign. At the last statewide meeting of town and ward coordinators on October 22, Robin Leeds announced the agreement and Jackson's upcoming gestures of support. The three hundred coordinators, mostly white male construction workers, rose as one and greeted Leeds's words with the loudest standing ovation of the day.

"There's still a lot of work that has to be done around minority issues and getting into the trades, but a lot of minority union members participated in this campaign at the grass-roots level," comments Richard Bolling, a member of Ironworkers Local 7 for nine years. "There is an automatic sympathy in the black community for people who are fighting for decent wages. I was in Dudley holding signs, and people would always honk their horns and hold their thumbs up. They don't make the money either, and they identify with the person in the trenches fighting for wages." Selma Johnson is a unionist and health-care organizer who coordinated the campaign in the Mattapan section of Boston. "I wore my button everywhere," she says. "People would stop me and ask about the issue. They may have thought there were problems getting into the unions, but they also understood that when you cut union wages, it starts a chain reaction for everyone."

Alex Rodriguez, Felix Arroyo, and a number of other political figures took the anti-repeal message to Hispanic voters through the Latino Democratic

Committee and numerous community organizations. The committee distributed Spanish-language literature in the growing Hispanic communities across the state. In a letter sent out to his supporters in Massachusetts, United Farm Workers leader Cesar Chavez wrote: "Question Two was placed on the ballot by the usual suspects—anti-union contractors, certain developers, and insurance interests. Their motivation never changes—it's greed. To them the best worker is an unorganized, underpaid worker."[24]

The persistence of the coalition-building effort among women and minorities paid off. A pre-election poll in the *Boston Herald* indicated that there was a "gender gap" on Question 2. Among men surveyed, 51 percent favored repeal, with 44 percent opposed, while 53 percent of the women opposed repeal with 29 percent in favor of it.[25] The results on November 8 certainly indicated that the African-American community had taken the union side. On Election Day, Boston's four predominantly black wards turned down Question 2 by an overwhelming 4 to 1 vote. There were other benefits that reached beyond the voting booth. "A forum for discussion was created, and new interchanges occurred," Robin Leeds concludes. "Relationships were established that hopefully laid a basis for future work."

The campaign also had an important impact on minority tradesmen and women in the field. "I've always been a union man," says Bolling, "but I got a new taste of brotherhood. In an era of conservatism, this was an amazing thing for the unions. Personally, I hadn't seen anything like it since the civil rights movement. Our unions became part of everyday events in the street and reminded people that unions are the best way to keep your rights from being taken away."

8 | Into the Breach

*I don't know how prevailing wage will
affect me, but I'm just tired of losing.
—Representative of a New Bedford
UAW Local, April 27, 1988,
speakers training session*

The Committee for Quality of Life sponsored four speakers' bureaus around the state in the last week of April. Although the themes and tactics of the campaign were still in their infancy, the training sessions offered the committee its first chance to present general strategic outlines to hundreds of trade unionists. "They helped clarify the issue," says Dick Courtney of the United Food and Commercial Workers (UFCW). "They suggested what the arguing points of the campaign were going to be, especially for a non–building trades person." No formal campaign literature was yet available, but CQL staffers passed out some preliminary fact sheets. "The handouts were useful," remarks AFSCME's Jonathan Tuttle. "I was able to put together some packets for my staff and local union members."

The April sessions represented the committee's initial outreach efforts. In February the AFL-CIO's four-page "Action Plan" had outlined an overall game plan and listed a series of goals to be accomplished by November. By the end of the winter, a campaign staff had been pulled together and outside consultants had been retained to oversee media activities and field operations. The committee had made an early determination that the field component of the campaign should receive significant attention. On February 19 Arthur Osborn sent a letter to all AFL-CIO affiliates requesting support for a grass-roots field operation. "In a tight contest," he wrote, it "could make the difference between winning and losing." In April Capital Services, the campaign's field consultant, proposed a wide-ranging plan complete with job descriptions and a list of tasks. The consultant also suggested that a calendar be developed with plans for pledge card drives, bumper sticker distribution, phone banks, direct mail programs, literature drops, sign-holding in public areas, and primary and Election Day poll coverage.[1]

The original plan relied on the formal AFL-CIO structure. Accordingly, each of the state's fourteen Central Labor Councils was instructed to designate someone to coordinate campaign activity in its geographical area. The CLC coordinator was expected to supervise coordinators appointed by each union to take responsibility within their local. In January the committee wrote to each union affiliated with the AFL-CIO and asked for the name of a campaign coordinator. In theory, the CLC-based approach was the best way to get a broad representation of organized labor. In practice, the structure was slow to get off the ground. The unions' lack of familiarity with statewide political campaigns hampered organizational development. In addition, many union leaders outside the construction industry were reluctant to set aside their regular responsibilities in favor of an issue that still appeared to be beyond their normal range of concerns.

The initial response inside the building trades was only marginally better. While a number of unions were able to build on their voter registration efforts, others were fumbling to get started. In March Leo Purcell was elected president of the Massachusetts Building Trades Council, replacing the retiring Tom Evers. Although Purcell did not technically take office until July 1, he began working on the campaign two months earlier. In his first week, Purcell established the framework of an organizational structure for the building trades. Purcell appointed six regional coordinators, each of whom was responsible for the geographical territory of two of the state's twelve local building trades councils. In a May 5 memo Purcell described their initial assignments as the overseeing of voter registration and the fifty-dollar member assessments.

"I spent all of May trying to sell the organizational plan to the local councils," Purcell says. "I was arguing that this was a great opportunity to reach out and get the membership involved. The first time I ran around the state, it was bad news. People had their doubts that this piece could go together. Our history of doing things collectively across the state wasn't that good, so there were doubters. I was confident the structure would work, but I knew it wouldn't automatically fall into place."

The formal structures—through the CLCs and within the building trades unions—may have been in place, but the campaign was taking shape unevenly. In the Pioneer Valley an informal steering committee of union leaders in and outside the building trades had been meeting since March on a weekly basis. "We have more of a history of working together out here," explains Joe Dart, who served as the regional coordinator for western Massachusetts. "So we took the central plan, used what we could, and expanded on it where necessary." In much of the state, however, individual unions were still struggling to put their own houses in order and were in no position to fold their resources into the statewide effort.

At the beginning of August, Painters District Council 35 freed organizer Bill Murphy to work on the campaign full time. Purcell assigned the energetic Murphy to be his liaison to the regional coordinators, a task that involved major responsibility for the field operation. "When I came on," says Murphy, "there was really nothing in place under the umbrella of the CLC structure. Leo had been banging away for months at the building trades on voter registration, the assessment, and membership lists, but the whole thing hadn't taken shape."

By early August, the names of 725 coordinators had been submitted to the Committee for Quality of Life by a variety of AFL-CIO unions. Campaign coordinator Mark Govoni assembled the lists at the committee's headquarters in Boston's North End, but they did not add up to a nascent organization. The local union coordinators had volunteered or been assigned to handle responsibilities within their local. Few were prepared to extend their activities beyond their unions. All of them had full-time daily routines and were either unable or unwilling to add on another, essentially full-time, job description.

At the same time, Purcell and Murphy were constructing the foundation of a campaign organization within the building trades. They had two advantages unavailable to Govoni. First, the prevailing wage issue had its clearest impact on those in the construction industry. Purcell recognized that the commitment of time and resources required to support a field operation would probably come from building trades workers. Their livelihoods were on the line, and they were the most likely to make the necessary sacrifices. Second, the building trades structure shifted the focus away from the local union coordinator. In Purcell's format, each regional coordinator directed a group of town coordinators, most of whom turned out to be rank-and-file construction workers. This system tapped new sources of enthusiasm and energy, the wellsprings of successful political campaigns.

"There came a point," Murphy remarks, "when we all realized there wasn't much of a CLC-based field. It varied region to region. In some areas the building trades worked hand in hand with the CLCs; in others it just wasn't happening. In order for the whole thing to work, we had to start with the building trades." Arthur Osborn describes the change in direction as a pivotal point in the campaign. "The original design wasn't flowing the way it should have," he comments. "The shift from the CLC to the regional coordinators came from Leo, and I concurred with it. It made the field operation really work."

Under the altered structure, the regional coordinators—Joe Dart, John Dutra, Harvey Isakson, Louis Mandarini, Jr., Bill Ryan, and Tom Williams—became "the cornerstones of the campaign," as Purcell put it. Each was responsible for his region. They could be and were held accountable for what did and did not take place. Still, any structure is only as effective as all of its component pieces. Before Labor Day, few of those requisite pieces were in place. In an August 29 letter to the leadership of the state's construction unions, Purcell wrote in frustration: "Many of you are to be applauded for your efforts. Unfortunately, and for the life of me I can't understand it, some of you have done nothing or next to nothing and it's starting to show."[2]

The purpose of Purcell's letter was to announce a September 9 meeting in Worcester. That gathering of more than a hundred building trades business managers and business agents proved to be an important step in unifying the unions' leadership for the final stages of the campaign. They unanimously agreed on a common formula for the assessment and established a deadline—October 1—to collect outstanding funds. Those financial decisions were critical since the campaign was running a deficit at the time. In addition, the union leaders collectively affirmed a measure already endorsed by several individual locals, that is, that Election Day would be an unofficial holiday for every union construction worker in Massachusetts.

If the September 9 meeting cemented the commitment made by the unions' leadership, a series of meetings the following week provided the basis for extensive grass-roots participation. Between September 12 and 14, more than two thousand people attended regional meetings in Boston, Lawrence, Pittsfield, Swansea, and Worcester. Any doubts about rank-and-file interest in the campaign were quickly dispelled. "Those meetings were a litmus test," says Joe Dart. "I was particularly pleased at the numbers of non–building trades people—as much as a quarter of our group."

Each meeting followed a standard format. After a

series of speeches, a committee staff person outlined a fourteen-point field plan that carried the campaign from September through Election Day. At the end of the presentations, the volunteers caucused by town and selected one of their ranks to serve as town coordinator. The selection process varied. In some cases, unions had already designated members to represent their particular trade in their hometown. For example, Waldo Banks of Ipswich arrived at the Lawrence meeting as the coordinator of the ironworkers for his town. Similarly, Bernadette Higgins had already volunteered to be the painters' coordinator for Medford. At the regional meetings, they simply took on responsibility beyond their trades and offered to oversee all the volunteers in their towns. In some situations, it was a matter of numbers. Rick Brown became the Gloucester town coordinator because he was the only person at the regional meeting who had lived in the town all his life. As her neighborhood's only representative, Selma Johnson took on the Mattapan section of Boston's Ward 18. Other choices were fairly arbitrary. "We had twenty-three people from Weymouth," laughs Martin Downey. "Everyone took one step back, handed me a pen, and I became the coordinator."

Inevitably, the selection process was imperfect. "Some of the people who initially took the positions didn't always follow through," comments regional coordinator Harvey Isakson. Few of the town coordinators had any conception of what the demands on their time would prove to be. "Ninety-nine percent of them had never been involved in any kind of politics or militant unionism," notes Jack Getchell, who supervised field activity in the Cape Cod area. The field endeavor ultimately rested on the shoulders of the town coordinators. Most of them worked full time on construction sites, then returned home and spent their evenings and weekends in meetings or on the phone cajoling, motivating, and ensuring that the seemingly endless list of campaign tasks was accomplished.

Most of the town coordinators grew into their roles. Some, like Gary Cesa, an Amesbury sheet metal worker, were laid off and chose to forgo a regular paycheck in order to work fulltime as coordinators in their communities. Dozens of other rank-and-file workers suspended their daily routines and devoted the bulk of their nonworking hours to the campaign. A few were overwhelmed by the enormous responsibility and were replaced by the regional leadership right up to the final weeks of the campaign. Ron Livingston of Rockport and Ed Harrison of Middleton, for example, did not take on the coordinator's job in their towns until early October.

The vast majority of the town and ward coordinators were union tradesmen and -women, but there were exceptions. "Some of the hardest-working people were not in the building trades," notes John Malone of Painters Local 257. The Cambridge coordinator was an electrician, but half of his city's ward captains were neighborhood activists, housing and tenant advocates, students, and other volunteers outside the labor movement. The Woburn coordinator was a schoolteacher. In Boston, Domenic Bozzotto, president of Hotel and Restaurant Employees Local 26, took responsibility for Wards 4 and 5. In the small town of Wendell, the lead position was filled by the Democratic party town chair, who also happened to be a non-union carpenter.

As the burdens of the campaign increased, each regional coordinator developed intermediate layers of leadership. Regions were broken down into manageable pieces of territories, and a number of the most active union officials were assigned to monitor a group of towns within each area. The rapidly evolving system improved communication from the towns to the state headquarters and back down again. But the final responsibility for the public face of the campaign lay in the hands of those who had chosen to represent the Committee for Quality of Life in their hometowns. "I'm convinced," says Nancy Doherty, a laborer from Lowell, "that our success depended on the personalities and effectiveness of the town coordinators." Bob Munro, business representative for Painters Local 39, agrees. "For years," he says, "our members expected the business agents to take care of things because that's what we got paid for. If it weren't for them, we'd have no prevailing wage right now."

The town coordinators built their committees based on lists of union building trades workers in their communities. The Committee for Quality of Life had instructed each local union to supply it with membership lists. The state campaign headquarters then sorted and shipped out the appropriate names to each town coordinator. Unfortunately, the lists were slow to arrive. As late as September 21, Purcell repeated his request for names from union leaders. "We have to supply [the town coordinators] with the troops," he wrote. Assuring the confidentiality of the lists, he continued: "I suppose that there could be several reasons why you're unable to provide us with your list, but I will give you one reason why you can't refuse. We can't win without it."[3]

By early October, most of the unions had complied. The Carpenters, for example, delivered a master list to the Committee for Quality of Life with a contact person in nearly every city and town in the state. The union then provided each of those people with the names of all the other carpenters in their community and instructed them to cooperate with (or even to become) a Quality of Life coordinator. Armed with these lists, as well as membership lists provided by the national AFL-CIO, virtually all of the town and ward coordinators were able to identify the union building trades workers who lived in their communities.

Coordinators typically held committee meetings in their homes. In areas with a significant working-class population, the committee size quickly exceeded living-room capacities. "I started with 8 people in late September and ended up with 125," says Jim McCormack, an operating engineer from Saugus. "We started meeting at the American Legion Hall after the crowd got too big for my house." The Quincy Quality of Life Committee included well over two hundred active members. The Weymouth committee had even more. "I have a tiny little house," Paula Downey says. "We'd put the kids to bed and have our meetings. There were so many people in the house that it was a good thing we had a front and back door for the overflow." Smaller communities proved to be just as active. According to John Dutra, regional coordinator for the southeastern part of the state, "There was a kind of friendly competition between towns that worked out well. People prodded each other to keep going."

The geographically defined character of the town committees cut against the grain of the basic format of the labor movement. Organized labor consists of dozens of organizations that represent workers on the basis of occupation or industry. Unions' geographical jurisdictions correspond to the locations of workplaces, not members' homes. While this structure makes sense for collective-bargaining purposes, it does not work as well for a statewide political campaign, which targets voters in their home communities. In most labor-based political activity, individual unions take responsibility for generating support from their own members for particular candidates or issues. Early on in the prevailing wage campaign, the Committee for Quality of Life determined that the mobilization and coordination of resources would require transforming the standard union-by-union solicitation of members into a field organization based on cities, towns, and wards.

"As craft unions," comments Jack Getchell, who was a member of an industrial union before he became a bricklayer, "we don't have permanent internal organizations, like a steward system in a factory. We had to create a new structure." Members of craft unions also had to overcome their traditional identification with their own trades in order to meld into cross-craft campaign organizations. On most construction sites of any size, trades workers tend to socialize at lunch or on coffee breaks with other members of their own craft. Yet buildings do get erected by a team of individuals with a variety of craft affiliations. The campaign required similar or greater cooperation—and under much more intense circumstances and within a briefer time frame.

In some cases, workers from one craft reluctantly responded to or took direction from members of another trade. Years of craft rivalries and jurisdictional disputes over job-related assignments did not vanish overnight. By and large, however, rank-and-file enthusiasm for cooperation in the town committees outpaced the union leadership's ability to set aside past differences. The urgency of the issue and the deadline of an election drove together trade organizations that had not had a history of strong working relations. For example, the participation of the Carpenters Union, representing one of the single largest blocs of organized workers in the construction industry, was critical to the campaign, despite their lack of affiliation with the state Building Trades Council. Historical divisions had to be overcome. As Martin Ploof, business agent of Carpenters Local 475 put it, "We knew the carpenters couldn't do everything, and the building trades couldn't do everything. But together we could."

"Working in the town committees was a lot like working on a construction site," says Waldo Banks. A campaign had to be built, a schedule followed, and individual assignments carried out in a team effort. Boston Ward 19 coordinator Paul Roche suggests that the positive working relations built up in the campaign carried over onto the job site. "At first there was some reluctance to cross trade lines," he says. "Then all the barriers broke down and people worked together. It was one of the best things about the campaign." Nearly all the coordinators reported the same experience. "For the first time, carpenters, electricians, plumbers, pipefitters, ironworkers, laborers, and the rest were all on one common ground," says Martin Downey.

At a certain point, the town and ward committee system superseded the union structure and developed a dynamic of its own. Each local union fed its resources into the overall effort. The grass-roots committees emerged as the principal organizational expression of the opposition to Question 2. Union officials simply made sure they kept up with the momentum of the committees. "I told our local's town coordinators to cooperate with the Quality of Life coordinators and give them as much time as they

Labor Day parade in Marlboro, 1988. Martin Ploof

Campaigning

"Salute to Labor" day at Heritage Park in Fall River, September 4, 1988

Bringing the campaign to a rally for clerical and technical workers at Harvard University. Constance Thibaut

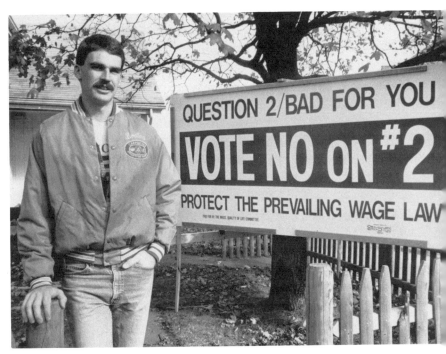

A carpenter campaigns in his front yard. Canton Journal

Inspired by the sight of Laborers Local 175 member Frank J. Rozmus standing on a Lawrence streetcorner for weeks on end with his sign, artist Gaitan Demers assembled this plywood sculpture. Gregory Muzerall

Statewide meeting of town coordinators, October 22, 1988.
Bill Doherty

Greeting motorists in Kingston. Daniel Zavalcofsky

Campaigning for commuters in Quincy, October 26. © 1988
John Bohn/Patriot-Ledger (Quincy)

November 1 labor rally in New Bedford. AFSCME Council 93

could," says Dana Kelly, organizer for Pipefitters Local 537. "Then I sent each of our members a list of all the Quality of Life town coordinators so they would know whom to contact in their town. That way every base was covered. I didn't want members coming to me on November 9 saying they hadn't been contacted."

For all the official union involvement, what stuck in the public's mind was the constant presence of individual campaign workers in their communities. They stretched this political contest beyond the modern conventions of tightly controlled photo opportunities and television sound-bites into a campaign based on grass-roots visibility and direct voter contact. Lasting impressions of the prevailing wage battle flowed out of the work of the town and ward committees. Three weeks before the election, *Boston Globe* columnist David Nyhan wrote of the campaign volunteers: "They do not wear suits, neckties, or shirts with starched white collars. They wear jeans or work clothes, collar turned up against the wind. Knuckles that held tools all day turn white with cold at day's end, holding sticks with placards. . . . [Their wages and benefits] represent progress not just for the construction workers, or for union workers, but for everyone who works for a wage."[4]

The success of the field operation was premised on the simple human arithmetic of the campaign. "Our biggest advantage all along was that we had people," says Bill Murphy. AFL-CIO staffer John Laughlin told an Attleboro newspaper a similar story: "People can put bumper stickers on their cars, people can walk with signs at rotaries, people can walk into voting booths. Corporations can't." Even the ABC's Stephen Tocco acknowledged this reality. "We're prepared to match them in a media war," he said, "but we know we're not going to be able to match them as far as organization, and we're not even going to try."[5]

As a former signpainter, Murphy took overall responsibility for the sign campaign. He developed formulas for regional distribution based on voter density and set the wheels in motion for a sign production mechanism. While the budget included funds for billboards and public transit signs, the plan focused on lawn and hand-held signs, which were produced and distributed by the Committee for Quality of Life. The placards were screened in New Bedford and Lowell by union shops that agreed to deliver them at or below cost as a gesture of support for the campaign. The committee received the raw signs and set up framing operations around the state to assemble them. Carpenter apprentices from Springfield's Local 108 framed most of the signs for use in the western part of Massachusetts. The Laborers' Training Center turned over their facilities in Hopkinton for sign production, and union halls in Fall River, Lowell, Quincy, and other communities all became mini–production centers. The demand for signs was so unyielding, however, that the burden of supply fell primarily on the Boston sign center. "By the end," recalls Rick Morgan, business manager of Signpainters Local 391, "we made ninety to a hundred thousand total signs. It was three to four times what we'd initially planned on."

Morgan coordinated the statewide day-to-day production and distribution of the signs from a vacant warehouse in South Boston. The structure was one of the buildings of an affordable housing complex financed by the Carpenters' First Trade Union Savings Bank and was slated to be gutted and renovated after the election. At the request of Robert Marshall, business representative of Carpenters Local 33, the developer agreed to make the fifty thousand square feet of space available for the campaign's use.

The skills of the building trades were quickly applied. Union electricians wired the building for the power tools required for sign assembly. Local 33 supplied a stream of apprentices and out-of-work carpenters to run the table saws, the radial arm saws, and the power miter boxes during the day. In the evenings, volunteers from other trades assembled the precut frames. "This whole operation was what unions were designed to stop," jokes Morgan. "It was a sweatshop, the most aggressive bunch of people I've ever seen. They policed themselves. At the end, we were going so strong that we had to assign a guy full time to repair broken staple guns."

Morgan's job was a logistical nightmare. Due to the constantly escalating volume of signs required and the competing demand from the presidential campaign, materials were in short supply. "We bought up every piece of posterboard in New England," Morgan notes. "We ordered wood strapping from New York City, Buffalo, and Albany. We went all the way to Chicago for corrugated nails. We must have used three-quarters of a million staples." As the campaign heated up, the warehouse crews expanded their shifts from eleven to fifteen hours, seven days a week. Unemployed volunteers spent the day; employed trades workers joined them before and after their regular jobs. While not so flashy as other, more publicized aspects of the campaign, the relentless work of the South Boston sign factory signaled the depth of the determination to defeat Question 2. "Whenever I'd get down in the dumps about how it was going, I'd go over to the sign factory," says Joe Walsh of Plumbers Local 12. "Then I'd think to myself, 'How can we lose?'"

"Vote No on 2" signs were everywhere. They appeared on the front lawns of triple-deckers and single-family homes, in the windows of apartment houses and small businesses, on the sides of commercial buildings, and in the hands of thousands of workers who regularly stood at street corners and major intersections. They soon rivaled the hundred thousand blue-and-white "Vote No" stickers that graced the bumpers of cars and trucks across the state. The blanketing of Massachusetts with the unions' message was apparent to everyone. Lieutenant Governor Evelyn Murphy told a union group: "Everywhere I went I saw your 'Vote No' signs." Even opponents grudgingly recognized the massive public presence of the union message. The author of an anti–prevailing wage op-ed column in the *Boston Herald* complained that nightly commutes out of Boston "took a lot longer than usual" because of the large numbers of sign-holders on Southeast Expressway overpasses.[6]

The town committees spread the "Vote No on 2" gospel in a variety of ways. On two separate occasions—the weekends of October 15 and 16 and November 5 and 6—volunteers distributed more than 1.5 million pieces of campaign literature to nearly every household in the state. No other political campaign in the history of Massachusetts had ever covered the state so thoroughly—let alone twice. Using maps provided by the committee, the town and ward coordinators broke down their communities street by street and assigned a given number of blocks to each volunteer. With sufficient numbers of volunteers, the system was straightforward and effective. Workers canvassed the town of Lowell, for example, in two and a half hours. Coordinators in rural areas adapted the plan to their particular needs. "We couldn't do the literature drops door to door in the Berkshires," says Pat Mele, Jr. "We went to shopping malls, bingo parlors, and all the dumps in the small towns where everybody gathers." Efficiency was not the only motivation for alternative distribution techniques. "In the remote areas, it's not just a matter of saving time," points out Jonathan Tuttle. "If you try to go to each house, you might get a 12-gauge shotgun in your face."

The Committee for Quality of Life designed a

"Dear Friend" postcard that was funneled through the town committees. The card contained a brief and concise argument against the referendum. The card was intended to appeal to friends, family members, and neighbors in a way that would be more personal than the more anonymous process of literature distribution. Space was left at the bottom of the card for each campaign volunteer to write additional comments. "I thought the cards were one of the most successful campaign items in terms of reaching out to people outside the House of Labor," Joe Dart argues. The town committees made extensive use of the program. Using holiday lists and family address books, campaign volunteers sent out nearly two hundred thousand postcards in a two-week period.

While the town committees took over much of the responsibility for local organizing, individual union halls turned over their copying machines, mailing machines, and telephones to the campaign effort. Some of the larger locals with more extensive resources served as secondary campaign headquarters, providing the space for mass mailings, phone banks, and nightly meetings—right on through to the victory parties. The daily tasks of monitoring job sites were put on the back burner. "At a certain point," notes the IBEW's Joe Sheehan, "we told our members to forget the little brush fires. We only got out to the jobs on an emergency basis."

Union offices proved particularly helpful as locations for phone banks. In the last month of the campaign, the Committee for Quality of Life staged a telephone-contact outreach effort. On September 30 Craig Stepno and Rich Rogers led a training session for a group of fifty union leaders who had volunteered to be phone bank supervisors. Stepno and Rogers explained the process and handed out a kit that included a set of instructions, "scripts" for phone callers, and a tally system to record the responses. The committee's plan first targeted the homes of AFL-CIO members in Massachusetts, followed by members of the general public if time allowed. As Stepno puts it, "We wanted to make sure our base—union households—never could say they weren't asked."

One hundred and twenty-five telephone lines either already existed or were newly installed in fifteen locations around the state. In the Merrimack Valley, Rudy Parent supervised five phones six nights a week for five weeks. Each trade in the area staffed the phones on a rotating basis. "We averaged about four to five hundred calls a night," says Parent. "As a result, we were able to get to the general voters' list after three weeks." The phone banks were also adapted to specific regional needs or used to back up the town committees. At times, some of the phone lines were devoted to reminding inactive building trades workers to join their local committees. Alternatively, supervisors often shifted the randomly targeted calls to communities with weak Quality of Life committees.

In all, a hundred thousand calls were made to union households, plus an additional seventy-five thousand to the general public. Stepno and Rogers also developed a "mom-and-pop" operation to supplement the union office–based phone banks. The larger town committees recruited volunteers who were willing to make calls from their homes, and the Committee for Quality of Life mailed them separate phone lists. "We got a few hundred more people involved that way," says Stepno. "We developed separate kits for them and showed them they weren't alone, that they fit into the big picture." The mom-and-pop phone operation provided additional opportunities for participation for nonworking family members and homebound sympathizers. "We had a guy in Billerica who is terminally ill with cancer," notes Dana Kelly. "He couldn't do the visibilities, but he burned up the phone lines."

By October the field operation was in full swing. The building trades unions in Massachusetts had achieved a newly found sense of unity and settled into the daily, and nightly, routine of an ambitious statewide political campaign. "I virtually shut down my normal responsibilities," says Tom Chirillo, business manager of Laborers Local 133. "I told the job stewards they had to be the business managers until after the election." The town committees, composed of union construction workers and a significant number of sympathizers, carried out the overall campaign plan piece by piece. "Where the committees were strong, it was just amazing," muses regional coordinator Bill Ryan. "They took on an energy by themselves. We just fed them the materials."

9 | Down the Homestretch

*The battle over a Prevailing Wage Law
that many people in Massachusetts
hadn't given a second thought just a
few months ago has eclipsed all other
political battles in the state for its
intensity and bitterness—grabbing
center stage in the upcoming
November election.*
—Boston Globe, *October 18, 1988*

The initial survey conducted
by Bannon Research, the
Committee for Quality of Life's pollster, indicated in
May 1988 that 49 percent of voters favored and 30
percent opposed repeal of the prevailing wage law.
There were a number of explanations for the tilt.
Most voters either knew little about the issue or
vaguely associated repeal with tax savings. The committee's campaign was still in its formative stages
and had not yet effectively challenged the ABC'c
claims. Furthermore, as Brad Bannon pointed out,
the wording of the ballot created substantial confu-

sion. The language was convoluted, and the question was framed so that a yes vote eliminated while a no vote preserved the law. Despite all these caveats, however, an obvious truth could not be overlooked: Bannon's springtime numbers confirmed the initial assumption that defeating Question 2 would be an uphill battle.[1]

Bannon's second survey, conducted in September, demonstrated the progress made by the Committee for Quality of Life. Forty percent of the respondents now opposed repeal, 23 percent were in favor, and a significant 37 percent remained undecided. The *Boston Globe* and the *Boston Phoenix* reported in the first week of October that the race was essentially a dead heat. The *Phoenix* termed it a "high-visibility contest that's apparently too volatile to call with confidence." The *Boston Herald*'s result more closely paralleled Bannon's figures. The October 5 edition of the *Herald* suggested that opponents of repeal were ahead 50 to 25 percent. Two weeks later, on October 19, the lead was holding relatively steady at 51 to 30 percent.[2]

The specific numbers may have been in dispute, but every political observer in Massachusetts recognized that the momentum had swung away from the ABC. The polls reflected the public visibility of the union's campaign, the impact of the Data Resources study, the Committee for Quality of Life's growing credibility with the media, and, finally, the committee's early and intensive television advertising between September 19 and October 2. In one of the

Television commercial produced by the Committee for Quality of Life simulated a newscast featuring an anchorwoman interviewing a hostile contractor. Courtesy Politics, Inc.

Sending a Message

★★★ THE REVIEWS ARE IN! ★★★

QUESTION 2 IS BAD FOR YOU! VOTE NO ON QUESTION 2.

★★★
WE MUST SUPPORT QUALITY CONSTRUCTION IN OUR CITIES AND TOWNS!

"In my experience, you get what you pay for. If we take the low bid, we want to know all bidders are using equally skilled craftsmen."

— Kathy Sullivan, Selectman, Town of Stoneham
★★★

WE MUST KEEP TAX DOLLARS IN OUR COMMUNITIES!

"Having a prevailing wage requirement helps workers and their families. But it also keeps the community thriving. A decent standard of living translates into stable local tax revenues."

— WBZ (TV) Boston

WE MUST KEEP MASSACHUSETTS WORKING MEN AND WOMEN WORKING!

"The only clear result of question #2 will be lower wages for Massachusetts residents and a lower standard of living for local workers and their families. The cost of repeal would be fiercer competition for local jobs from out-of-state contractors and less money spent in local small businesses."

— Independent Economic Study by Data Resources, Inc. of Lexington, MA.

WE MUST GUARANTEE EQUAL PAY FOR EQUAL WORK!

"It is ironic that as the construction trades are opening up to women seeking jobs, the owners should try to repeal the long standing prevailing wage structure which provides a decent wage."

— Molly Yard, President National Organization of Women
★★★★★

WE MUST PAY SKILLED CRAFTS-PEOPLE AN ADEQUATE WAGE!

"The average wage for a Massachusetts construction worker in 1987 was $26,734."

Bureau of Labor Statistics, U.S. Department of Labor

FINAL SHOWING — A POLLING PLACE NEAR YOU!
VOTE NO ON QUESTION 2, NOVEMBER 8th.

Authorized and paid for by the Committee for the Quality of Life, 215 Hanover St., Boston, MA 02113

In a temporary "sign factory" set up in South Boston, union members worked around the clock to manufacture signs. John Gillooly

This advertisement ran in newspapers throughout the state. Courtesy Committee for Quality of Life

Stacking signs at the South Boston warehouse. John Gillooly

Some of the 100,000 signs ready for distribution. John Gillooly

campaign's more important tactical decisions, the committee opted for a "first strike" advertising approach, despite the shortage of funds in the early fall. "We had to buy the airtime early on, even though the money hadn't yet come in," Arthur Osborn says. "But we went ahead and decided on early TV. We tried to flip the issue so the building trades weren't the special interest. We wanted to paint the ABC as the special interest."

In the analysis of his October 19 data, *Herald* pollster Gerry Chervinsky suggested that the committee's advertising campaign had, in fact, helped reframe the debate on Question 2. Repeal advocates, he said, had a "very winnable fight" but had been outmaneuvered by the union side.[3] "We were able to preempt them on the tax-savings question," concurs Leslie Israel, president of Politics, Inc., the media consultant for the campaign. "We had to make them the bad guys and take the tax issue away. It was a two-step strategy. First, we wanted to undermine the ABC's credibility and convince the public that they were no good. Second, we wanted to show that we were everyone's friends and neighbors, reinforce our side as the 'good guys.'"

The committee launched the ad compaign on September 19 with two spots produced by Politics, Inc. Both lasted sixty seconds, longer than the standard thirty-second political message. "The issue was complicated," explains Israel. "We wanted the time to do something both catchy and substantial." In one of the ads, the host of a game show titled "What's

Your Motive?" challenged a wealthy contractor's position opposing the prevailing wage law. Recalling the ineffective suspension of the Davis-Bacon Act under President Nixon, the host reminded the audience that this "is the quiz show that wants to know what's in it for you." As the host and guest sparred, the spot ended with a voice-over answering the title–question: "The motive is profit."

The committee also aired an ad with a newscast format in which a news anchor interviewed a shady-looking contractor. As the anchor questioned the contractor's claim that repeal would mean tax savings, the blustering contractor blurted out: "If I can just import some cheap labor from out of state, then I can make more . . . . I mean . . . then you can save tax dollars!" The ad closed with the anchor turning and speaking to the audience: "It's a good law and a fair law. Don't be deceived."

The ads' high production values, their broad humor, and their attacks on the contractors eroded the ABC's standing. "The two ads moved us up quickly in the polls," Israel notes. They also sparked a controversy that would shadow the campaign. Two of Boston's three network affiliates refused to play the simulated newscast spot. Despite the obviously satirical nature of the ad, officials of WCVB-TV (Channel 5) and WNEV-TV (Channel 7) suggested that viewers would not be able to distinguish it from an actual newscast. WBZ-TV (Channel 4) and ten other television stations in the state aired the commercial with a disclaimer.

In many ways, WCVB's decision was unsurprising. While political candidates are guaranteed access to paid radio and television ads, federal law permits media outlets to refuse without explanation advertisements for referendum questions. As a longtime advocate of prevailing wage repeal, the station had shown little sympathy for this or any other union cause. In November 1987 WCVB endorsed the ABC's signature drive. On September 23, 1988, the station began running pro-repeal editorials in which Vice-President and General Manager S. James Coppersmith intoned: "The prevailing wage is ripping us off."[4]

The ABC tried to take advantage of the stations' anti-union stance. On October 4, the Fair Wage Committee charged the Committee for Quality of Life with the use of "deceptive" ads and called on state Attorney General James Shannon to investigate whether there were grounds for a criminal prosecution of the CQL for false advertising. Hours later, Shannon rejected the charges. In a statement released by his office, the attorney general wrote: "It is particularly reprehensible to make false accusations of criminal misconduct for political purposes."[5] Despite the rapid rejection of the ABC's charges, the stage was set for a continuing and bitter battle over paid advertising.

Having accomplished its preemptive goals, the Committee for Quality of Life limited its expenditures for the first two weeks in October to less expensive radio time in order to save the remaining media budget for the final three weeks of the campaign. The Fair Wage Committee, on the other hand, was forced into a defensive position when it released its first set of commercials. "We went with an ad package," Tocco told reporters in mid-October, "because our opposition is out there convincing people that we're nothing but a handful of contractors who want to make more money." In order to defuse the greedy contractor image, the ABC's ads relied on pro-repeal statements from Barbara Anderson of Citizens for Limited Taxation and Mary Hale, a selectwoman from the small town of Tyringham and president of the Massachusetts Municipal Association.[6]

Anderson and Hale repeated the principal ABC campaign themes, but their nearly identical statements also reflected a growing concern with the impact of the union ads. "The construction unions pretend just contractors care about this issue," their scripts read. "They're wrong. We care." With the claim that repeal would mean tax savings under increasing scrutiny, these and all subsequent Fair Wage Committee commercials shifted thematic gears. They sought to deflect the charges of employer greed by turning the tables and pinning responsibility for the high costs of construction on the employees. Anderson and Hale both decried the supposed state-guaranteed $26-an-hour wage scale for painters, despite the fact that the union rate in Massachusetts ranged from a low of $16.16 to a high of $21.25.

The Fair Wage Committee's commercials slowed

the rapidly rising fortunes of the Committee for Quality of Life, but momentum had already been established. The emergence of the CQL's field organization, coupled with the effectiveness of its commercials in September and October, infused the campaign with a growing sense of confidence. "When we started with the bumper stickers, we couldn't give them away," Tom Williams says. "Then it got so hot that people were grabbing them out of our hands." The "Vote No on 2" message was getting out in the media, through community organizations, and on the street. The town committees were growing on a daily basis. "I knew things were changing when people started to call me instead of the other way around," comments Weymouth coordinator Martin Downey.

October 11 was the last day for new voters to register for the general election. The turnout of new voters across the state reflected the interest generated by the campaign. City and town officials reported the highest level of new registration in twenty years. More than two thousand people registered in Brockton on the final day. Seven hundred stood in line in Milton. "I would say frankly what's bringing them out is Question 2," said a Kingston registrar that night. "There are a lot of people in the trades."[7] Quality of Life town committees sent representatives to registration sites to argue against the referendum. Four hundred Question 2 opponents rallied in Quincy and leafletted new registrants until the city hall closed at 10 P.M.

The Committee for Quality of Life scheduled five statewide "visibility" days during October and early November. Town and ward coordinators organized their volunteers to hold signs at major intersections before and after work. In communities with large committees, coordinators went beyond the state program. Anti–Question 2 signs and literature appeared at virtually every parade, town fair, and gathering of significant size in Massachusetts during the fall of 1988. One night two weeks before the election, members of some of the North Shore town committees passed out twenty-seven thousand pieces of literature to commuters at Boston's North and South stations. The Quincy committee handed out six thousand leaflets every night for weeks at subway stops in their community.

"Our people were shy at first," says Tom Williams. "Then they really got into it." Campaign activists sought endorsements from city and town councils, boards of selectmen, and local newspaper editorial boards. They talked about the consequences for local communities of residents' reduced purchasing power. "This affects everyone, the guy at the corner store," said laborer Ron Glennon. "If I make less, I can't buy as much."[8] The presence of local working men and women appealing to political leaders in their communities carried significant weight. After a group of Question 2 opponents crowded an Ipswich Board of Selectmen meeting on October 24, the board dropped its planned endorsement of the referendum and voted to take no position. "The local people who spoke were the most powerful part of that whole meeting," says Phil Mason, who coordinated activity in all the North Shore towns, "because they brought the campaign home."

Building trades workers sought out reporters and filled the letters-to-the-editor columns in the state's newspapers in the last weeks of campaign. "I'll go stand on any corner I have to," Steven McDonough told the *Globe*. "I used to work at the Quincy Shipyard, and I know what it's like to lose wages. I don't want to go down that road again." Electrician Paul Thibault wrote to a Lynn newspaper: "This is not a Democrat vs. Republican or Union worker vs. non-Union worker issue. It is an issue of the average working person vs. For Profit Employers." Supporters of the prevailing wage law outside the labor movement expressed similar sentiments. As Holly Hingston-Cahill wrote to the *Globe*: "A no vote on Question 2 isn't a vote for the unions. It's for all of us. Unless, of course you own the company."[9]

The months of media effort by the CQL campaign staff, supported by the chorus of voices from the grass roots, produced both expected and unexpected endorsements. A gradually swelling number of local and state officials held daily press conferences opposing the referendum. A surprising number of media outlets with little history of sympathy for unions ultimately called for the defeat of the ballot question. Those who supported the referendum invariably faced extensive criticism. At a Greenfield rally on October 28, State Representative Carmen Buell waved a clipping of a local pro–Question 2 editorial and angrily accused the newspaper of suggesting that "people who work with their hands should not be paid decent wages." In the biggest prize of all, on October 18 the *Boston Globe*, the state's largest and most influential newspaper, reversed its position of many years and editorialized against Question 2.[10]

The debate over the referendum permeated political discourse. *Globe* rural columnist Peter Anderson devoted a Sunday column to the issue, despite the fact that, as he put it: "I have avoided writing things of substance. . . . I write little stories about people like my friend Burt who walked into his big garden on Summer Island, Maine, early this summer to find a deer inside the high fence." On this occasion, however, Anderson exchanged his customary light fare for a serious discussion: "Tax savings is not what this ballot question is really about. This is a class issue. I wonder if the people who object to union painters making $21 an hour also object to corporate executives who make $1 million a year plus another half-million in bonuses. . . . If we see union abuses, it is because union work is more visible. We do not see the abuses hidden behind corporate doors and glibly explained by lawyers whose hourly wages are an offense to good reason. . . . If the strength of this country lies in its working people, what happens when we lower their wages? I will vote for the working man, for the rich are adept at taking care of themselves."[11]

"In the last six weeks of the campaign, something

clicked," says veteran organizer Janice Fine, who served as a field coordinator for the Committee for Quality of Life. "People went the extra mile. They picked up whatever opportunities we gave." The pace of the campaign hit a fever pitch. "My mind was running wild," recalls Martin Ploof. "How many different places could you put signs, how many organizations could you reach out to, how many people could you send the 'Dear Friend' cards to?" A flood of volunteers held signs on street corners, worked the phone banks, and helped to send out mass mailings. "We were putting together a last-minute mailing," Bill Murphy says. "I told Martin Walsh [of Laborers Local 223] we needed some bodies, and immediately three guys show up. An hour later we needed some more. I asked Martin again, and I turned around and there are fifty people licking envelopes."

"This campaign was different from any other I've worked on," Fine claims. "At a certain point, it transcended the field plan. The campaign tapped into a constituency that was more than ready to be mobilized. They mobilized themselves. We just tried to keep up with the demand. It was an organizer's dream, something you just can't structure. It's the point at which an organization turns into a movement, when people just go off on their own."

The field organization had been a family affair from the beginning. Spouses and children joined building trades workers in distributing literature, holding signs, sending "Dear Friend" cards, talking to neighbors, and carrying out other campaign activities. "The participation of families was the difference in the community feeling of the campaign," suggests Larry LaFlamme, business agent of Roofers Local 33. Certainly, the highly visible presence of ordinary working families challenged the ABC's attempt to paint the Committee for Quality of Life as little more than a crowd of cigar-smoking labor leaders. "Having your neighbor instead of a politician ask for a vote was very effective," Frank Coco of Laborers 175 points out. Many campaign participants believe it was the most crucial piece of the entire effort. "I sincerely feel the reason we defeated Question 2 was due to family and friends of the tradesmen," insists Kathy Dineen, wife of the Sherborn town coordinator.[12]

Faced with a unified and growing army of building trades workers and their supporters, ABC strategists opted to counterattack with cruder and more direct assaults on union workers. In the last month of the campaign, the Fair Wage Committee material dwelled on the purported $50,000 income level of construction workers and indignantly complained about overpaid building trades employees. One ad resurrected the controversy over the Great Barrington landscaping contract. In spite of the subsequent information that contradicted the Fair Wage Committee's original claim that the prevailing wage law had multiplied the costs of the Great Barrington contract by a factor of five, the commercial presented the unchanged "horror story." The thirty-second spot did manage to add a new, and somewhat ugly, twist by portraying a supposedly typical worker in sneakers and shorts who lazily pushed a lawn mower with his feet while reclining on a park bench.

Another commercial continued the attempt to pit public sector employees against construction workers by featuring a teacher, a nurse, and a policeman while a voice-over discussed relative wages. Medford schoolteacher John O'Brien was shown standing by a chalkboard while the $50,000 figure for construction workers was contrasted to a teacher's salary of $28,000. Unfortunately for the ABC, O'Brien proved to be an unwilling television star. At an October 31 press conference organized by the Committee for Quality of Life, O'Brien told reporters that he had allowed the filming as "a courtesy." However, he went on, "I made it quite clear that I did not wish to appear in any film that could be used as an anti-union appearance. . . . I state unequivocally that I do not condone or support the message of the commercial I was seen in."[13]

Despite the distortions of fact, repeated exposure to the ABC's negative images of workers began to have an impact on the public. "We had come from behind and were doing well," Arthur Osborn notes, "but the polls were showing slippage because of their hard-hat ads." The ABC commercials received heavy airplay over the weekend of October 29 and 30. On Monday morning the top leadership of the Committee for Quality of Life held an emergency meeting and elected to prepare additional material. "We wanted to give the viewers real live warm working people, instead of the ABC's image of a cold hard hat," Osborn says.

With just over a week left before the election, there was little time to produce a new ad for television and get it on the air quickly enough to have an effect. A hurried call was issued for a young, telegenic construction family to be filmed the following day. "We normally don't script for people, but we didn't want actors," Leslie Israel comments. "It wouldn't have worked as well or been as real." Politics, Inc., prepared a script and set up for a shoot on Tuesday morning.

Three families were asked to read the statement for the cameras. The producers selected the version featuring ironworker Alan Carpenito, who had been active in the campaign, and his family. The commercial was simple, effective, and intended to underscore the reality that the vast majority of union construction workers face lives of danger and economic insecurity. In the ad, Alan Carpenito said: "I get mad when a bunch of rich contractors say I make big money. Why do they lie?" His wife, Lynne, a former construction laborer, added: "We're just barely able to make ends meet."

The Fair Wage Committee had hung the $50,000-sign on the campaign. Continuing protestations that U.S. Department of Labor statistics clearly indicated that construction workers in Massachusetts averaged less than $27,000 a year had not deterred the

ABC from repeating its inflated claim. The commercial was designed to make the committee's number real, to flesh it out in the words of a working construction family. "It was a great ad," bricklayer Paul Deane says. "It was me and my life."

It was not, however, the Carpenitos' life. Since 1980, Alan and Lynne Carpenito had purchased five rental properties, renovating them after work and on weekends. In the frenzied Massachusetts real estate market of the 1980s, the values of their houses had increased to a total of $1.2 million by the fall of 1988. At the time of the filming, the Carpenitos had mentioned that numerous elements of the script did not correspond to their own lives. The Carpenitos were assured the discrepancies did not matter. Under the rush of a deadline, the media team failed to screen any of the three families thoroughly and chose not to consider the potential damage of contradictions between the video image and real life.

It would not have mattered had the information about the Carpenitos' real estate holdings not become public. But it did. On Thursday, November 3, two days after the ad was filmed, the Fair Wage Committee held a press conference and handed reporters packets containing copies of deeds, mortgages, and photos of the five houses. Fair Wage staffers had a field day mocking the union side. Barbara Anderson commented acerbly: "They apparently couldn't find any poor, underpaid, struggling union workers."[14] The Committee for Quality of Life's worst fears were realized the following morning. The bottom half of the front page of the *Boston Herald* was covered with a large headline and a story on the controversial commercial.

"I was devastated," recalls Nancy Doherty. "I was stunned," says Martin Ploof. "It was like finding out God had had an affair." With only four days to go before the election, there was no time to repair the political damage. For many, the credibility of the campaign's message was in jeopardy. The Committee for Qualify of Life had managed to convince a significant portion of the electorate that the image of the overpaid construction worker was false and that the campaign truly spoke for everyone who struggled to make a decent living. Committee activists now feared that the controversy over the commercial would simply reinforce a generalized public cynicism about all things political and that a campaign that had been perceived to be on the side of the angels would be considered just one more example of "politics as usual."

The consequences for voters were considerable, but not so severe as the impact on the men and women who had put their hearts and souls into the campaign. "It was a self-inflicted wound that did more damage to us than to the general public," says Bill Ryan. "It took the steam out of our people because they had made the investment." Union office and campaign telephones rang off the hook. Rank-and-file members felt hurt and angry and showered campaign staffers and union leaders with bitter complaints. "I took a pounding on the phone," recalls Jack Kelleher ruefully. "A lot of our people felt betrayed." No one begrudged the Carpenitos their good fortune; the callers simply questioned the process that resulted in their selection to represent the campaign.

"The message was right; the messenger was wrong," Arthur Osborn wearily told reporters in the wake of the controversy. Frustration over the blunder was compounded by the knowledge that thousands of campaign volunteers could easily have been the appropriate messengers for that particular message. "That ad was my story," says electrician Bill Corley, expressing a widely held sentiment. The flap over the ad temporarily complicated outreach efforts. "I worked the phone banks that whole weekend," says laborer John Croucher. "Late Sunday afternoon, the guy next to me reached a woman who asked him about the five houses. He said, 'Believe me, if I owned five houses, I wouldn't be here all day calling people up.' "

The Committee for Quality of Life quickly withdrew the commercial. By the end of October, the entire television strategy of both sides had become a morass of charges and countercharges. The Fair Wage Committee originally demanded that the Carpenito ad be removed from the air, then turned around and used footage from the ad for a commercial of its own. The Committee for Quality of Life, on the other hand, pointed out that the ABC ads with John O'Brien and the inaccurate account of the Great Barrington town contract were fraudulent distortions. In addition, CQL attorneys argued that the Fair Wage Committee's unauthorized use of footage from the Carpenito ad violated copyright laws. Ultimately, a number of outlets refused to run any of the ads under dispute. A Boston television station official told the *Herald* that the misrepresentation of fact and the negative tone of the commercials were "unprecedented." He continued, "We've never seen anything like this."[15]

With the election only a few days away, campaign workers focused on the remaining tasks. A *Boston Globe* poll published on Sunday, November 6, had deepened the gloom. The survey showed the pro-repeal side leading 49 to 38 percent and suggested that the "biggest gains were among voters who described themselves as moderates or conservatives or who earned between $30,000 and $50,000."[16] "That's when the town coordinators really showed their colors," says Tom Chirillo. "They had to re-rally all these construction workers who were down in the dumps. And they did." The committee had scheduled final pre-election activities for the evening of November 7. Across the state, town committees mounted their most impressive displays of opposition to the referendum. Motorists heading south out of Boston faced an astonishing sight. Stretching from South Boston through Dorchester to the Quincy border, a line of hundreds of Boston activists, separated by, at most, a few feet, held "Vote No on 2" signs. The line was picked up in Quincy and continued, with some interruptions, on arterial roads paralleling the twisting coastline through the neighboring communities of Weymouth, Hingham, and Hull. "A lawyer I know drove down from Boston," Tom Williams smiles. "He told me it looked like Hands Across the Sea." The field organization had regained its stride. "When all was said and done," John Malone concludes, "the main thought left with the voters was the contrast of local people writing letters and holding signs versus a big, hostile, nationally connected organization."

The election-eve visibility was a dress rehearsal for the following day. Late in the evening and before dawn the next morning, campaign volunteers made sure that signs were in place to welcome voters as they headed for the voting booths. Town and ward coordinators had already assigned shifts to committee members to ensure complete poll coverage throughout the day. By 7 A.M. at least one (and usually many more) Committee for Quality of Life volunteer stood outside virtually every polling place in the state with signs, literature, and Election Day "palm cards" printed in both English and Spanish. "Voting crowds were heavy," reported a Worcester newspaper, "but there were few workers for candidates and issues to be seen. The exception was the small army of union members urging people to vote against the proposal to repeal the prevailing wage law."[17] On November 8 the army numbered more than twenty thousand statewide. With union construction sites shut down in Massachusetts, an infusion of first-time volunteers from the building trades

Standing outside the polls on election day. Harry Brett

Election Day and Election Night

Election day in Boston. Harry Brett

At the polls. Harry Brett

Father and daughter on election day in South Boston. Arthur Pollock, Boston Herald

Reporter interviewing Arthur Osborn, president of Massachusetts AFL-CIO, on election night, before the returns were in.
Harry Brett

Despondent proponents of Question 2 watch the returns at Burlington headquarters, November 8, 1988. (L-R) Francis Faulkner, assistant director of Citizens for Limited Taxation (CLT), Stephen Tocco, executive vice-president of ABC, and Barbara Anderson, executive director of CLT. Yunghi Kim, Boston Globe

Victory party at the Park Plaza Hotel, Boston. (L-R) Arthur Osborn, Leo Purcell, president Massachusetts Building Trades Council, Bill Murphy, organizer Painters District Council 35, Bob Haynes, secretary-treasurer Massachusetts AFL-CIO, and Nancy Mills, director Service Employees International Union Local 285. Harry Brett town basis. In addition, Stern identified a few hundred key precincts that made up a representative sample of the total electorate. As a result, the computer was able to interpret the total vote in those communities and predict the ultimate outcome within one or two percentage points.

Channel 5's claim at 9:53 P.M. of a victory of 55 to 45 percent for Question 2 was the first public prediction of the final result. "I went crazy when I saw that on television," recalls Paula Downey. But by ten o'clock, the tallies of the committee's predictor precincts clearly indicated that the ballot question was going down in flames. "When we saw the television report, we couldn't believe it," recounts regional coordinator John Dutra. "We already had results in from Acushnet and some precincts in Fall River and New Bedford. We knew what was happening." As individual precinct results continued to flow into state headquarters, campaign staffers in Boston happily informed the incoming phone callers that the statewide pattern was proving to be favorable. Channel 5's prediction was quickly discounted as subsequent television reports recognized the accuracy of the committee's findings. By 11 P.M. committee officials at the Park Plaza Hotel in Boston had declared victory.

The victory parties at the union offices, community halls, and restaurant function rooms around the state were hardly scenes of wild celebration. The campaign volunteers and their families were exhausted. Most of them had started the day at five or six in the morning and had worked continuously into the evening. The strain of months of extensive activity in unfamiliar terrain on behalf of an issue with significant implications for their livelihoods had taken its toll. Relief, rather than the exhilaration of victory, defined the collective mood at the gatherings. In Ashland union officers of Carpenters Local 475 disposed of the leftover pizza and soda and closed their building at 12:10 A.M., after the last key precinct reported in. Harvey Isakson, regional coordinator for central Massachusetts, attended the more boisterous victory party at the Polish-American Club in Worcester. Nearly eight hundred campaign workers jammed the hall. "I left early because it had been a long day," he remembers. "And I had to go to work in the morning."

10 | Building the Future

Unions in Massachusetts did
something they have rarely done in
modern times—widely identified
themselves as the working men
and women living next door.
—Boston Globe, *November 10, 1988*

I am extremely proud to have had a
small part to play in this grass roots
effort of democracy in action . . . [but
I am] still angry that we were put in
the position of asking our neighbors
and residents of the cities and towns
we live in to please not destroy our
quality of life. . . . I am angry that
every time someone comes up with an
idea of how to cut taxes, it is always
by cutting wages. No one says for
instance, "Let's cut profits," or "Cut
the cost of material or land cost, or
legal cost or financial cost or
consulting cost."
—*Letter from William McDonough,*
  Chelmsford town coordinator,
  Chelmsford Independent,
  December 1, 1988

In November 8, 1988, the voters of Massachusetts endorsed the state's prevailing wage law. The decision-making process inside the voting booths, however, had little to do with the details of monitoring publicly funded construction projects. Even after the extensive educational campaign, few of those who pulled the "no" lever could have explained fully the intricacies of the legislation under dispute. The Committee for Quality of Life had succeeded in redefining the ballot question to embrace issues that transcended Chapter 149 of the General Laws of Massachusetts. What caught the voters' interest was the larger question of the nature of employer–employee relations in contemporary America. The vote became, in effect, a referendum on workers' rights and corporate greed.

Question 2 came hard on the heels of eight years of an administration that gave new emphasis to the idea that what is good for business is good for the nation. Ronald Reagan, the most explicitly ideological president of the post–World War II era, built his economic policies on the premise that the road to public salvation must be mapped out in corporate boardrooms. The business community took full advantage of the administration's policies as they drove this route to unparalleled financial rewards. In the past decade, the average chief executive officer's compensation grew at a 12.2 percent compound rate, while the number of millionaires more than tripled between 1983 and 1986.[1]

In fact, Reagan's pro-business fiscal, monetary,

and legislative policies only accelerated the global trends that have reshaped the American economic landscape and its class structure since the early 1970s. The weakened position of the United States in international markets and the replacement of moderately paid manufacturing jobs by low-paid service employment predated Reagan's 1981 inauguration. Reagan's seminal contribution was to personalize and legitimize the unfettered search for individual private wealth that characterizes the typical operations of latter-day American capitalism. The results of the decade that lionized Frank Lorenzo and Ivan Boesky are now clear. The downward strain on middle-income earners has swelled the ranks of low-income families. Seven out of every ten Americans who moved out of the middle-income range between 1978 and 1986 were forced into the low-income category. Furthermore, the gap between rich and poor is still growing at an alarming rate. According to a recent congressional report, families whose earnings ranked in the top fifth gained 24 percent more income between 1973 and 1987. Those in the bottom fifth suffered an 11 percent decline in income.[2]

Under the Reagan administration, the bouquets delivered to employers were complemented by brickbats for workers. The firing of the air traffic controllers in Reagan's first year in office set a new standard for anti-unionism at the federal level in the modern era. Subsequent legislative initiatives, Department of Labor rulings, and appointments to the National Labor Relations Board continued a consistent policy of hostility toward existing and potential union members. By the end of Reagan's two terms, most studies revealed that the public increasingly resented the discrepancy between the treatment accorded employers and that accorded employees. The timing of Question 2 coincided with declining support for Reagan's policies, despite his continued personal popularity.

"By November 1988," says John Dutra, "people may have had enough of corporate America's coming after labor." There was no guarantee, however, early in 1988 that the battle to defeat Question 2 could tap this pool of populist, anti–big business sentiments. Two critical myths had to be shattered before the issue could be redefined. First, voters had to perceive the Associated Builders and Contractors for what it was—an organization of employers, not of advocates for sorely pressed taxpayers. Second, voters had to recognize who construction workers actually were— the working men and women next door who shared many of the same problems all working people do, not a gang of overpaid, underworked hard hats. Both tasks were accomplished, and the result was a historic electoral victory. As Paula Downey puts it, "We got a sympathetic vote because people came to understand our lives."

Those lives were on display every day in the final months of the campaign. While the high degree of visibility of prevailing wage supporters certainly affected the electorate, it thoroughly changed the way many of the campaign's participants think of themselves and their ability to affect the world around them. Conversations with campaign activists resonate with declarations of new-found pride, a sense of accomplishment, and pleasant surprise at the amount of political power they were able to wield. "The victory elevated our people's opinion of themselves," claims David Dow. "We gained faith in and respect for each other, not to mention a new-found respect from politicians." Not everyone enjoyed the unyielding pressure of political campaign deadlines. For some, it was a series of arduous tasks that had to be accomplished. "I spent a lot of time in the rain with my first-grader," Waldo Banks points out with some irritation evident in his summing up. "I'm mad we had to work so hard for something that was so right."

For the most part, though, the opportunity to take a stand outweighed the personal sacrifices. "This was the first time I'd ever done *anything* like this," says Bill Rossiter, a member of Elevator Constructors Local 4 who served as the Topsfield town coordinator. "It's made me a lot more active and aware." The campaign uncovered talents and a depth of commitment that few of the volunteers knew they had. People who are most comfortable with tools and manual tasks found themselves engrossed in the kinds of discussions ordinarily reserved for political strategists. IBEW Local 103, for example, held regular meetings for their coordinators. "They would report on the progress in their communities," says Rich Gambino. "The members were testifying as if it was an AA meeting." Phil Mason's recollection is similar. "At the first meeting I went to, I was afraid people would be bored stiff. But it went on for an hour and a half, and not a soul left the room."

"When I was an apprentice, few political issues were ever brought to my attention," Dana Kelly of Pipefitters Local 537 notes, "but our apprentices rallied to this cause and took part in a statewide campaign. They've learned what our opposition will do, that they'll lie to get laws repealed." Over the course of the campaign, increasing numbers of union hats, T-shirts, and jackets cropped up on job sites. Union members expressed a stronger identification not only with the issue at hand but also with their labor organizations in general. "The campaign forced all of us to identify ourselves in our communities," comments Bill Ryan. "Now our neighbors know us as union members, not just through the PTA or the Little League."

With the close of the campaign, business as usual returned to the construction industry. Workers concentrated on the tools of their trades, union leaders refocused on the daily tasks of monitoring job sites, and buildings continued to be erected. But nothing is ever exactly the same after a campaign of such major proportions. Attendance is higher at building trades union meetings in Massachusetts since the fall of 1988, and more questions are asked. "The attitude in my local has changed," reports Pat Walsh, business manager of Laborers Local 223 in Boston.

"The members now feel that if they stick together they can accomplish a lot. There are construction workers in every ward of the city that can give any politician a battle."

As membership involvement increases, so do members' expectations of their leaders. The large-scale grass-roots participation in the Question 2 campaign boosted the general membership's interest in and sophistication about the broader issues facing the building trades unions. "A lot of the members are asking, 'What's next?'" claims John Dutra. "They're telling the leadership, 'We did it, we built the foundation. Now you finish the house.'" The blueprints of the house, however, remain to be drawn. The electoral victory set the ABC on its political heels, but non-union employers still play a majority role in the construction field. "The ABC won in one sense," comments Joe Dart. "We were preoccupied by the prevailing wage fight and totally distracted from our business for a year and a half. As a result, their people got a lot of projects. Now we have to organize those unorganized contractors." The campaign may have demonstrated the potential power of a united labor movement, but it provided no clear-cut strategy for the building trades unions to reestablish their influence in the industry.

"Question 2 gave our unions the experience of working collectively, but we had an obvious goal and a fixed deadline," notes Leo Purcell. "The entire leadership had to get involved and had to include their members. But the challenge of turning around our industry will be tougher than the campaign. The problems are so big that they can't be wrapped up in a political slogan. There's disagreement at the leadership level that can stop people from working together. Not everyone is convinced that there is a clear collective answer. In some ways, all that's changed in the aftermath of Question 2 is that we have an experience under our belts that we can draw on."

Organized labor's predicament has been amply documented. Representing a shrinking percentage of the work force, the labor movement risks being written off as obsolete and politically irrelevant. The building trades are no exception to this rule. "If we don't continue to change quickly," Purcell warns, "we could be in serious trouble." The crisis in unionism cuts across every sector of the work force, but construction has a particular set of issues that must be addressed. In recent years, elements within the historically conservative building trades unions have begun to take a harder look at the obstacles to survival and growth. Change and renewal continue to be slow, but the critical state of affairs has lit a fire under the once-slumbering unions. New initiatives—corporate campaigns, coalition efforts, political action, and beefed-up organizing campaigns—now surface more frequently across the country.[3] In Massachusetts, the state Building Trades Council launched a comprehensive "Building Our Future" campaign in late 1989 that draws on these strategies as well as the kind of membership involvement Question 2 evoked.

The battle to defeat Question 2 can serve as a model for campaigns elsewhere, but even in this apparently clear-cut victory, the difficulties of the real world intrude. Despite the electorate's verdict, the letter and spirit of the Massachusetts prevailing wage law remain vulnerable. According to Bill Murphy, "We saved a law that wasn't being enforced, and it's still not being enforced." As an organizer for the Painters Union, Murphy knows the statute and its implications as well as anyone in the state. He knows that there is one very simple reason why most painting work on state-funded jobs is currently being done by non-union contractors—the risk of violating the law can be outweighed by the potential profits to be made.

"The prevailing wage law, along with other fair labor standards, is routinely violated in public construction," acknowledges James Snow, commissioner of the Department of Labor and Industries (DLI) in Massachusetts.[4] The continued existence of the law and DLI's best-faith efforts do serve as deterrents. But penalties for failure to file accurate payroll records or failure to pay the mandated rate are minimal. More important, the depleted number of DLI inspectors, attorneys, and other related personnel has made comprehensive enforcement difficult. And finally, even those cases that are investigated and ultimately prosecuted often founder on unresolved interpretations of the legislation. After two years of doggedly pursuing H. M. Horton Company, the largest non-union painting contractor in New England engaged in public construction, Murphy provided state officials with a full set of witnesses and a wealth of information demonstrating Horton's clear skirting of the law. In May 1989 an appeals court judge overturned a prior decision and issued a finding of not guilty based on a technical ruling that the prosecution had not proven beyond a reasonable doubt that the owner was aware of his own company's practices.

Non-union builders have learned the obvious lesson from this and similar rulings. The combination of an understaffed enforcement agency and temporizing justices signals that ignoring the law may be a sound business practice. The current situation offers a potential gold mine for non-union contractors, who are not bound by a collective-bargaining agreement. They feel free to pay employees far below the prevailing rate, pay "under the table," or subcontract portions of the work at lower wages and simply declare they know nothing about subcontractor employment practices. Fines of from $100 to $500 and even the more severe debarment procedures amount to slaps on the wrist in terms of potential gains. As it stands, a system designed to create a level playing field for all contractors, union and non-union alike, can promote precisely the opposite effect. The illegal payment of substandard wages reduces total costs and provides a bidding advantage to non-union contractors relative to organized employers, who must pay the union scale. "With the job going to the low bidder, they can have it every time as long as they think they won't get caught," Murphy concludes. Despite the voters' demonstration of support for the prevailing wage standard, a significant number of non-union builders continue to believe the law can be safely and rewardingly ignored.

Stricter enforcement of the prevailing wage law is an important piece of the building trades unions' overall agenda, but it is by no means the only or the most important piece. Ultimately, union standards will define conditions in the construction field when unions once again come to represent the majority of the work force. Therefore, to the extent that any single issue most clearly embodies the unions' future, it is organizing. A foreign concept for many construction unionists a decade ago, organizing is now widely recognized as the difficult, but necessary, task ahead. This means both "top-down" organizing—convincing contractors to sign union agreements—as well as "bottom-up" organizing—appealing directly to unorganized construction workers. While it may be standard fare in industrial and service-sector unions, bottom-up organizing represents a new direction for many building trades unionists, who have long held that the best guarantee for job protection in an unstable industry is a limit on union membership.

The focus on organizing has sharpened in the aftermath of the electoral victory. The day after the election, IBEW official Richard Monahan told a reporter, "We're going to knock on the doors of [ABC contractors'] employees" as part of organizing drives.[5] Several unions used their campaign materials as vehicles to reach out to unorganized workers. Plumbers Local 12, for example, sent out twenty-two thousand letters on Question 2, reaching every licensed journeyman and registered apprentice plumber in Massachusetts. "We also used it as the basis for future organizing by including separate 'further interest' cards," notes Kevin Cotter. "We got a *lot* of responses." These contacts will lay the foundation for union organizers as they seek to organize workers firm by firm. The victory on Question 2 also increased organizers' credibility in advocating the value of unionism. "During the summer of 1988," points out Dana Kelly, "a lot of contractors didn't want to sign up with us because they were convinced we would lose. Since November 8, we've been contacted by both employees and owners who recognize our strength. Now we can do both bottom-up and top-down organizing."

The campaign created new opportunities and taught lessons. "We had an overall strategic plan and followed it to the end," concludes Bob Banks of Ironworkers Local 7. "If we had gone the way we normally do, reacting step-by-step, we would have been killed. Now we have to establish a better permanent system to get information out and involve the members." A number of locals have begun the process of institutionalizing the grass-roots structure that was developed during the campaign. IBEW Locals 102 and 223, for instance, have implemented a "Zip Committee" structure that could grant considerable autonomy and responsibility to rank-and-file members. Under this system, electricians who live in each zip code of the locals' jurisdiction will represent their unions on local political issues and community outreach. In addition, they can serve as surrogate organizers by approaching non-union electricians in their towns.

Another of the campaign's mechanisms that can be continued and strengthened are the ties formed with groups outside the building trades. "The building trades have a fierce independence and a narrow scope," notes Tom McIntyre. "The lesson to be learned from the campaign is the wisdom of working with the larger labor movement. It has a longer and stronger history of working with community groups than we have. We need to develop these associations even further through involvement with issues like affordable housing and homelessness." Dana Kelly explicitly links further outreach efforts with obligations from the campaign. "We need to pay back the people who helped us who didn't have to," he contends.

Of all the relationships nurtured over the course of the campaign, the most fragile remains the one between the building trades and organizations representing minorities and women. Some of the relations established in the fall of 1988 have continued. On March 14, 1989, the Boston Building Trades

Council and the Contractors Association of Boston, an organization of minority building employers, co-sponsored a breakfast attended by two hundred union officials, contractors, community activists, and political leaders. The breakfast followed a January Supreme Court ruling that jeopardized public policies aimed at encouraging minority and women contractors. Joe Nigro, general agent of the Boston Building Trades Council, told the gathering that, despite the Court's action, the unions fully supported the concept of affirmative action and the set-aside programs enacted by the city of Boston. He described the unions and the minority community as participants in "a joint quest for social justice."

Boston's Painters District Council 35 adopted coalition tactics as part of its drive to stop the city's major hotels from using itinerant, non-union painting contractors from out of state. Council Secretary–Treasurer John Simmons launched a labor–community alliance to demand that hotel owners respect Boston's residency hiring requirements as well as affirmative action and set-aside practices. "We believe that a coalition is the best vehicle for improving training and job opportunities for local residents," said Simmons. Bill Fletcher, chair of the Community Task Force on Construction, described an April 6 press conference to announce the coalition as "a historic moment." Citing national conservative trends, Representative Augusto Grace labeled the unions "a beacon in the wilderness."[6]

Tensions built up over decades do not disappear

overnight, and there will be numerous tests of the relationships that emerged during the prevailing wage campaign. In particular, state and city officials are urging the building trades unions to admit large numbers of additional urban residents, minorities, and women into their training programs as part of the major public works initiatives that will be started in the 1990s. While union officials have endorsed the state programs, many are apprehensive about the timing of the admission of a substantial number of new entrants in light of rapidly rising unemployment figures in construction as the Massachusetts building boom of the 1980s grinds to a screeching halt. Still, the nature of the discussions that are underway represents a qualitative change from previous years. As Bill Fletcher put it, "What we're looking for now is a new and equal partnership that responds to the concerns of both sectors."[7]

The opportunity to create a genuine partnership has implications far beyond the construction industry in Massachusetts. While the need for change may be particularly glaring in the building trades, a willingness to speak out forcefully in opposition to racial and sexual discrimination is not always uniformly demonstrated throughout the labor movement. If unions intend to rebuild their declining membership rolls, they will have to include, on the basis of sheer numbers alone, more of the growing percentage of the work force made up of women and people of color. More important, if organized labor intends to advocate economic justice for all working people, its credibility hinges on its ability truly to represent everyone who works for a living.

The Committee for Quality of Life performed its function and is now essentially dormant. "This was a single issue effort," argues Paul L'Heureux. "This manpower and effort will not be turned out for anything else." Certainly the unprecedented scope of the campaign is unlikely to be repeated. The direct economic threat posed by the repeal movement, the drama of a battle over workers' rights, and the historical moment all added up to a unique set of circumstances. On the other hand, the campaign clearly boosted union political involvement in Massachusetts. Participation in the labor delegation at the 1989 state Democratic party Issues Convention reached an all-time high, in part due to the continued activism of some of the CQL's town and ward committees. "We learned with Question 2 that we can't do it alone," insists Robert Haynes, secretary–treasurer of the Massachusetts AFL-CIO. The AFL-CIO's four-point "action agenda" for the 1989 convention reflected this perspective with its support for public education, affordable housing, a clean environment, and equal opportunity in the face of racial and sexual discrimination. Similarly, the AFL-CIO has been a principal supporter of the Tax Equity Alliance of Massachusetts (TEAM) in its campaign to advocate fair taxes and the retention of decent public services in the face of overwhelming tax- and service-cutting pressures to address the 1989–1990 $1 billion-plus state budget deficit.

Why was Question 2 defeated? In its simplest terms, a frustrated Fair Wage Committee spokesman's postmortem is as good a starting point as any: "We were simply outspent and outorganized."[8] The explanation offered by Jim Braude of TEAM goes somewhat further: "The Committee for Quality of Life fought on the merits of the issue. They didn't sidestep the tax question; instead they directly said that there would be no savings. As a result, the fact that this was a workers' issue and a class issue was never hidden." Perhaps the lesson to be learned is that the labor movement will arrest its decline and reassert its potential when it once again—as it has done in its finest hours—identifies unions with the desires and aspirations of the entire working community and with the broader crusade for social and economic justice. Unions have their greatest appeal when they simultaneously serve the daily needs of their members and incorporate a larger vision that can attract potential new members and the general working public. The resurrection of a democratic, militant, broadly defined and class-based brand of unionism can lay the foundation for a reinvigorated labor movement.

The campaign to defeat Question 2 indicated the value of participation in the electoral arena, but most of labor's issues have been and will continue to be fought in the workplace and at the bargaining table. The terrain may be different but many of the principles are the same—creative strategies, membership involvement, collective action, an awareness of the changing composition of the work force, and a fusion of labor's concerns with the public interest. Recently, the labor movement in Massachusetts has generated a number of local union campaigns that incorporate these elements. In 1988 Hotel Workers Local 26 in Boston, for example, expanded the standard definition of collective bargaining by negotiating for a Housing Trust Fund that addresses the membership's needs for adequate and affordable housing. After many years of persistent organizing with a message tailored to university employees, the Harvard Union of Clerical and Technical Workers signed its first agreement with Harvard University in 1989. Later that year, the centerpiece of a three-month strike by Nynex employees, represented by the International Brotherhood of Electrical Workers and the Communication Workers of America, was a successful refusal to accede to the telephone company's demand that workers pay a share of health insurance costs. Each of these contract battles captured the public imagination by linking workers' efforts to broader social concerns. And within the building trades, Ironworkers Local 7 adopted the techniques of direct action and civil disobedience in November 1989 when 150 union members were arrested protesting the use of a non-union steel erection company on a downtown Boston construction site. As labor's problems mount, such innovative and militant strategies increasingly filter into mainstream union activity.

The underlying principle involved in the changing labor movement is inclusion—the inclusion of current members in union activities as well as the inclusion of the concerns of working people who currently stand outside the House of Labor. "Democracy in our unions may be a pain in the ass sometimes," comments Jack Getchell of the Bricklayers, "but it's our strong point. During the campaign, unions that operated on a top-down basis didn't respond as well. People need to have a tradition of being involved in order to take initiative." The Question 2 campaign demonstrated the remarkable impact of an inclusive brand of politics and unionism. "For years, the labor movement has been a movement of leaders," says carpenter Steve Joyce. "This campaign was different. It was grass-roots and showed the need for internal education, democracy, and membership involvement in order to reach out to the general public to combat the image of labor as a 'special interest.' "

expanded the ranks of the town committees. In addition, large numbers of members of other unions and community organizations served as poll watchers for the day.

From the state headquarters to the local communities, the committee created a system to troubleshoot any problem that might arise on Election Day. The regional coordinators established headquarters in the six major areas as well as an additional group of offices in the subregions. Most town and ward coordinators arranged for someone to staff their home phones. Calls regarding transportation to the polls, voter challenges, or legal questions were handled at the local level if possible, and, if not, referred up the chain of command. Coordinators toured the polling places in their jurisdiction, carrying coffee and words of encouragement and checking to see that coverage was adequate.

"We had about 80 percent of our people assigned beforehand, and then shifted the other 20 percent around during the day," says regional coordinator Bill Ryan. In many areas, the large number of volunteers allowed the luxury of three-to-four-hour stints. In others, coordinators shifted bodies and plugged holes as the day wore on. Margaret Blood supervised the hectic operation in the city of Boston. "If there was something that needed to be done," she marveled, "people would appear as if by magic." By choice or necessity, countless numbers of unionists spent the entire day at the polls, lobbying one last time for a no vote.

"Around noontime, we got the sense that things were going our way," says John Malone of the Painters Union in Springfield. "We were still uncertain, but all the workers in the field were celebrating. They could just tell by the reaction they were getting at the polls." Poll watchers across the state reported similar experiences. Nancy Doherty worked in the Merrimack Valley. "All day the voters were very responsive," she says. "We got a lot of thumbs-up. I had a good feeling."

By late morning, the constant ringing of telephones had slowed. "I was very fidgety," remembers Paul Deane. "I was staring out the window, wondering." For those at the center of the campaign, the weeks of nonstop activity were little more than a blur. It was all coming to an end, and their economic futures hung in the balance. "At a certain point in the afternoon, there was really nothing left to do," Tom Williams says. "It was like waiting for a kid to be born." Technically, the polls closed at 8 P.M. but the heavy voter turnout meant that complete reports of results were still hours away.

The Committee for Quality of Life had asked precinct captains to remain at the polls until the votes were tallied. As the returns were posted, each captain called his or her regional coordinator at one of the many victory parties held around the state. Each coordinator, in turn, telephoned the committee's "boiler room" operation at the Plumbers Union hall in Boston. A computer program, designed by consultant Alan Stern, tabulated the results on a town-by-

Notes

Chapter 1

1. *Evening Gazette* (Worcester), November 9, 1988.
2. *Union-News* (Springfield), October 29, 1988.
3. *Wall Street Journal*, October 24, 1988.
4. *New England Real Estate Journal*, June 24, 1988.
5. *Boston Phoenix*, October 7, 1988.
6. Upper-income communities are defined as those where the per capita income was above $14,200 in 1985; low- and moderate-income communities, as those with a per capita income below $14,200. Figures are from the Massachusetts secretary of state's office.

Chapter 2

1. *Daily Times Chronicle* (Woburn), April 25, 1988.
2. House Committee on Education and Labor, *Report on Davis-Bacon Amendments*, 100th Congress, 2d session, February 9, 1988, p. 15.
3. Bureau of the Census, *1982 Census of Construction Industries* (Washington, D.C.: Government Printing Office, 1985).

211

4. *Davis-Bacon Handbook* (Washington, D.C.: Building and Construction Trades Department, AFL-CIO, 1979).

5. *Massachusetts General Laws Ch. 149, Sec. 26.* See also, memorandum from Alec Gray to Attorney General James Shannon, August 19, 1987, in author's possession.

6. *Congressional Record*, 96th Congress, 1st session, July 27, 1979.

7. Ibid.

8. Thomas O'Hanlon, "The Unchecked Power of the Building Trades," *Fortune*, December 1968, p. 102.

9. *Congressional Record*, 94th Congress, 2d session, January 11, 1976.

10. "Coming to Grips with Some Major Problems in the Construction Industry" (New York: Business Roundtable, 1974), pp. 52, 19.

11. *The War on Wage Protection: The Business Offensive* (Washington, D.C.: Center to Protect Workers' Rights, 1979), p. 12.

12. *Engineering News-Record*, November 22, 1973, p. 43; May 3, 1984, p. 28; November 8, 1984, p. 68.

13. Mark Erlich, *With Our Hands: The Story of Carpenters in Massachusetts* (Philadelphia: Temple University Press, 1986), p. 224.

Chapter 3

1. *New York Times*, December 5, 1978.

2. *Carpenter*, June 1979.

3. Quoted in "The Davis-Bacon Act: Consideration During the 97th Congress" (Washington, D.C.: Congressional Research Service, 1982), p. 7.

4. *Carpenter*, July 1982; *Washington Report*, June 8, 1982, pp. 1, 20; *Builder and Contractor*, March 1984.

5. *Carpenter*, July 1982; *AFL-CIO News*, June 17, 1982; *Engineering News-Record*, January 10, 1985.

6. *The Davis-Bacon Act Should Be Repealed* (Washington, D.C.: General Accounting Office, 1979), p. 100.

7. March 10, 1978, letter quoted in *The War on Wage Protection*, p. 64.

8. *Salem Evening News*, August 31, 1988; *Boston Globe*, August 2, 1983; *Boston Business Journal*, October 7–15, 1985.

9. Statement of Representative Stephen W. Doran, February 15, 1983; State House News Service article, April 22, 1985; *Boston Business Journal*, October 7–15, 1985.

10. *Merit Shop Bulletin*, October 1985, p. 3.

11. Ibid.; Tocco testimony before the State Administration Committee, April 13, 1988; *Boston Business Journal*, August 22, 1988.

12. *Merit Shop Bulletin*, October 1985, p. 3; figures are from the Massachusetts Department of Labor and Industries, Division of Apprenticeship Training, 1988; for actual figures, see p. 101.

13. Minutes of the Prevailing Wage Coalition, December 29, 1982.

14. Minutes of the Committee for Local Option on Contracts, May 26, 1983; *Merit Shop Bulletin*, October 1985, p. 4.

15. *Boston Herald*, February 16, 1989.

16. Fair Wage Committee news release, December 2, 1987.

Chapter 4

1. Massachusetts State Carpenters Convention Proceedings, 1968, p. 12.

2. Stephen Krasner, "Barely Holding Our Own in a Rising Market," unpublished manuscript, 1988.

3. *Daily Item* (Wakefield), March 18, 1983.

4. *Boston Globe*, April 23, 1985.

5. Ibid., November 16, 1985.

6. Bureau of National Affairs, *Construction Labor Report* 13, no. 1557 (December 4, 1985); *Merit Shop Bulletin*, July 1987; State House News Service release, September 15, 1987.

7. *Boston Globe*, October 20, 1987.

8. Citizens for Fairness in Public Construction news release, August 5, 1987.

9. *Engineering News-Record*, October 22, 1987; *BTEA Newsletter*, November 2, 1987.

Chapter 6

1. *The Union Leader* (Manchester, N.H.), September 20, 1988.

2. Foundation for Economic Research, "The Peculiar Prevailing Wage Law," March 1988 (Needham, Mass.).

3. *Boston Herald*, May 17, 1988; Bryant Jordan, "Waging War Over Wages," *Business and Economic Review* 1, no. 8 (June 1988): 4–8.

4. *Boston Globe*, April 23, 1988, June 12, 1988.

5. *Boston Herald*, October 18, 1988.

6. Data Resources, Inc., "Study of the Economic Impact of Repeal of the Massachusetts Prevailing Wage Law," August 18, 1988. The DRI report was not the only new piece of economic ammunition to become available to the Committee for Quality of Life. In a column in the *Berkshire Eagle* (Pittsfield), economic development specialist Werner Elsberg drew on Bureau of Labor Statistics

studies to challenge the assertion that lower wages equal lower costs for a community. That argument, he wrote, "is misleading because it ignores the issue of productivity, quality, tax losses from lower wages and the multiplier effect of reduced wages" (September 12, 1988).

7. *Boston Herald*, August 26, 1988.

8. *Berkshire Courier* (Great Barrington), July 21, 1988.

9. *Evening Gazette* (Worcester), October 6, 1988; *Boston Globe*, October 18, 1988.

10. *Blackstone Valley Tribune* (Whitinsville), September 21, 1988.

11. *Boston Globe*, June 12, 1988.

12. Ibid.; *Boston Herald*, October 18, 1988.

13. *Taunton Daily Gazette*, November 4, 1988; *Standard-Times* (New Bedford), November 1, 1988.

14. *Cape Codder* (Orleans), November 4, 1988; *Sunday Herald News* (Fall River), November 6, 1988.

15. Quoted in Jordan, "Waging War Over Wages."

16. *Patriot-Ledger* (Quincy), September 20, 1988; statement by Jim Braude, executive director of the Tax Equity Alliance for Massachusetts (TEAM), September 29, 1988.

17. *Banker & Tradesman* (Boston), September 28, 1988; *Sunday Republican* (Springfield), September 25, 1988.

18. *New England Real Estate Journal*, August 26, 1988; *Transcript-Telegram* (Holyoke), August 9, 1988.

19. *Boston Globe*, June 12, 1988; *Medford Daily Mercury*, June 20, 1988.

20. *Patriot-Ledger* (Quincy), September 20, 1988.

Chapter 7

1. *Engineering News-Record*, August 18, 1988, p. 17.

2. *Transcript-Telegram* (Holyoke), August 9, 1988.

3. *Medford Daily Mercury*, June 20, 1988; *Berkshire Eagle* (Pittsfield), October 15, 1988; letter to the *Standard-Times* (New Bedford), October 5, 1988.

4. *AFSCME 93 News*, March–April 1988; *NAGE Reporter*, Summer 1988; *Salem Evening News*, June 13, 1988; *Transcript-Telegram* (Holyoke), August 9, 1988.

5. *Boston Phoenix*, October 7, 1988.

6. *Berkshire Eagle* (Pittsfield), October 26, 1988.

7. *Voice* (Shrewsbury), October 27, 1988.

8. *Harvard Crimson*, October 26, 1988.

9. Press release by John Thomas Flynn, October 25, 1988.

10. *Wakefield Daily Item*, August 18, 1988; *Boston Globe*, October 18, 1988.

11. *Transcript-Telegram* (Holyoke), August 9, 1988; letter from Denise Maher, president of the Massachusetts Tenants Organization, to Arthur Osborn, September 16, 1988, in author's possession; *Boston Business Journal*, October 31, 1988.

12. *Boston Business Journal*, October 31, 1988.

13. *Malden Evening News*, July 11, 1988; *Boston Business Journal*, October 31, 1988; *Boston Ledger*, September 30, 1988.

14. IBEW Organizing Department, "Union Organization in the Construction Industry," October 1988, p. 7.

15. Social Policy Research Group, "An Assessment of Construction Industry Employment Developments in Massachusetts and the City of Boston," June 1988, pp. 53, 61, 62, 67.

16. Social Policy Research Group, "Building Tomorrow's Boston: Affirmative Action in the Local Construction Industry," May 1988, pp. 27, 45.

17. Ibid., pp. 34, 38.

18. Statistics are from the Massachusetts Department of Labor and Industries, Division of Apprenticeship Training.

19. Taken from a Committee for Quality of Life quote sheet.

20. Quote is from an SEIU 285 campaign flier.

21. Bernadette Higgins, "Women . . . Take It Personally!" *Sojourner* 14, no. 2 (October 1988): 10–11.

22. Letter from Augusto Grace to Arthur Osborn, October 21, 1988, in author's possession.

23. For a detailed account of the negotiations, see Jeff Crosby, "Labor, the Black Community, and the Vote No on 2 Campaign," *Forward Motion* 8, no. 4 (December 1989): 6–15.

24. Letter from Cesar Chavez to UFW supporters in Massachusetts, October 6, 1988, in author's possession.

25. *Boston Herald*, November 7, 1988.

Chapter 8

1. Letter from Arthur Osborn to AFL-CIO affiliates, February 19, 1988, and Memorandum on Field Activities from Capital Services to the Committee for Quality of Life, April 27, 1988, in author's possession.

2. Letter from Leo Purcell to all business managers and business agents of Massachusetts construction unions, August 29, 1988, in author's possession.

3. Ibid., September 21, 1988.

4. *Boston Globe*, October 18, 1988.

5. *The Sun Chronicle* (Attleboro), October 17, 1988.

6. *Boston Herald*, November 9, 1988, October 24, 1988.

Chapter 9

1. Bannon Research, May 1988 poll for the Committee for Quality of Life.

2. Bannon Research, September 1988 poll for the Committee for Quality of Life; *Boston Globe*, October 1, 1988; *Boston Phoenix*, October 7, 1988; *Boston Herald*, October 5, 1988, and October 19, 1988.

3. *Boston Herald*, October 19, 1988.

4. *Commercial Bulletin* (Boston), October 7, 1988.

5. *Boston Globe*, October 5, 1988.

6. Ibid., October 14, 1988.

7. *Brockton Enterprise*, October 12, 1988.

8. *Patriot-Ledger* (Quincy), October 27, 1988.

9. *Boston Globe*, October 18, 1988; *Daily Evening Item* (Lynn), October 27, 1988; *Boston Globe*, October 30, 1988.

10. *Recorder* (Greenfield), October 29, 1988; *Boston Globe*, October 18, 1988.

11. *Boston Globe*, November 6, 1988.

12. Letter from Kathy Dineen to author, January 4, 1989.

13. *Boston Herald*, November 1, 1988.

14. *Evening Gazette* (Worcester), November 4, 1988.

15. *Boston Herald*, November 5, 1988.

16. *Boston Globe*, November 6, 1988.

17. *Evening Gazette* (Worcester), November 9, 1988.

Chapter 10

1. *Boston Globe*, April 11, 1989.

2. Steve Brouwer, *Sharing the Pie* (Carlisle, Pa.: Big Picture Books, 1988), p. 5; *Boston Globe*, May 15, 1989.

3. See "Up Against the Open Shop: New Initiatives in

the Building Trades," *Labor Research Review* 7, no. 2 (Fall 1988).

4. Quoted in Bob Banks and Mark Erlich, "Prevailing Wage Law Still an Issue One Year Later," *Boston Globe*, November 27, 1989.

5. *Patriot-Ledger* (Quincy), November 10, 1988.

6. *Boston Herald*, April 7, 1989; Painters and Allied Trades District Council 35 press release, April 6, 1989, in author's possession.

7. Painters and Allied Trades District Council 35 press release, April 6, 1989.

8. Dan Soyer, director of the Massachusetts Municipal Association, in the *Patriot-Ledger* (Quincy), November 10, 1988.